Memoirs of a French Courtesan

Volume 4: Payback

Memoirs of a French Courtesan

VOLUME 4: PAYBACK

Céleste Mogador

Translated by Kristen Hall-Geisler

Practical Fox, LLC
Portland, Oregon

Copyright ©2026 Kristen Hall-Geisler

Translation by Kristen Hall-Geisler
Original title: *Mémoirs de Céleste Mogador*
Translation copyright ©2026 by Practical Fox
All rights reserved

Paperback ISBN 979-8-9903034-4-7
ebook ISBN 979-8-9903034-5-4
Mogador, Céleste
Memoirs of a French Courtesan
Volume 4: Payback

Neither artificial intelligence nor large language models were used
to translate, edit, or design this work.

Practical Fox, LLC
Portland, Oregon
www.practicalfox.com

46

Leaving (continued)

My state of depression had reached the attic of my soul, and I would have killed myself to remove the pain if not for the letter that I received from the people who were caring for my adopted daughter. The woman had fallen dangerously ill, and they told me they could not keep the child. I spent a restless night and was on the road at daybreak.

The poor little angel had started to talk; she called me mother. I brought her back to my place. I clasped her against my heart and tearfully asked her if it was true that one day she would disapprove of me. Poor little thing! She couldn't understand, but she put her arms around my neck and kissed me, saying, "I love you, godmother."

I had no right to die. If God sent this innocent creature to me, maybe it was to give me a reason to right all the wrongs I'd done.

⁂

Two days later, three men came to my house to seize a sum of forty-six thousand francs that Robert owed to his jeweler as collateral that'd he'd so foolishly put up. I'd always been appalled by loans and those who held them. Lenders always appeared in my imagination with thick mustaches, stout canes, and ugly hats. I became almost crazed with fear and worry.

I wanted to write to Robert, but I threw down the pen in a rage. "Non!" I said. "I will be more generous than he was. I will not drag him back into this. It's better that there's nothing left to me but my tears. We'll be far from this damn city. I'll work so I can bring you up, my little Caroline. I've gotten out of the habit, but so much the better! The pain will be worth it."

I put on a veil and went to my theater, where I was in *The Queens of the Balls*. I danced and sang with a dead soul, but I had long since gotten used to this show. I'd spent my whole life in a masquerade like this. The necessity of it made me the most depressed creature. I'd believed I'd escaped this kind of life, so the idea of backsliding made my heart drop.

I was done with my scenes at nine o'clock. As I was leaving for home, I saw a man in the alleyway. He slid like a shadow along the walls and seemed to be fleeing from me. I quickened my pace, because his face rang a bell. I planted myself in front of him.

It was Robert, looking pale and defeated. His eyes,

usually so alert, were clouded with sadness. But sarcasm was still on his arrogant lips.

"Don't you try to avoid me," I said. "You owe me an explanation. I may have been to blame, but you don't have any right to torture me the way you have been. Only God has final judgment. You cannot take off and leave me with the idea that any man under heaven damns me. Besides, you already got your wish—your curses have come true. I'm being sued in a case that has nothing to do with me. I'm going to leave civilization as miserable as you are." My tears cut through my voice.

He showed me into a carriage and escorted me home. "I'm afraid of what's to come," he said, "and that's what brought me back to Paris. My assets were sold for half their value. Not only am I broke, but I'm still in debt."

"Yeah, me too. They came after me, saying that what is mine is yours. It's scandalous, because they know very well that's not true. But they say, 'A woman like that, we'll get a good price for her.'"

"Make liars of them! Céleste, defend yourself with all the energy and intelligence you possess! You have your rights, and there are judges. I would succumb to bitter regret if I knew you were upset. I would enlist as a soldier, but I'm too old. I'm thirty-three. I'm headed for the ends of the earth—Australia. Maybe I can live, as so many others do, far from France, asking nothing of anyone, not making a show of my misery for them. That's all I want. I'm out of ideas. I'm going to go wherever the ship takes me."

He stayed at my place. We paid for all our past joys with long nights of tears.

A letter from Berry pulled us from the abyss. They wanted to seize my house and furniture. I was told that they were going to come after the imaginary payment they thought Robert had given me.

Everything fell apart at once. I would see it come to desperation.

The unfair accusations that had been heaped on me in the past came back to mind. I was so depressed, I in turn heaped them on Robert with interest.

"Great!" I said to him. "You who only had insults and contempt for me, who wished me ill, or in the hospital, or in prison—you can leave happy. Go. We're done. If one thing gives me any consolation, it's that I told you what would happen between us. You piled gorgeous things on me, and you owe me justice. The challenge is in forcing your arrogant self to make a promise. Get out! Leave me alone with my despair. I will not blame you. You get to keep your family. The only things I get to keep are misery and torture."

Robert stared at me without saying a word. He sized up my willpower. It must have looked unmovable to him, because he slowly left, taking my words as an order of exile.

I went to see a legal representative who gave me the address of a lawyer. I prepared myself for the storm that was coming. To weather this new crisis, I called on all my courage. Knocked down a hundred times, I got back up with supernatural strength. I was called before the court.

My enemies, who seemed vulnerable, thought they were so great in dragging me through the mud. They took my past and published it so that everywhere I went, it got there first. They trampled my heart so often that I became cruel. I thought only of vengeance. Then I was annihilated, again, in my powerlessness.

I left my apartment on rue Joubert for the duration of the trial. If the judges were going to fall for falsehoods, I didn't want to be run out of my house. I couldn't labor under the illusion of safety. The battle that was being prepared would be long and difficult. It would be bitter.

I rented a little house and garden on avenue de Saint-Cloud for my daughter, who needed fresh air. All the women I had known danced around my downfall like witches. I didn't want to give them this joy. I tried to fool them—and fool myself and the anxiety in my heart—by making a show of my life of luxury and pleasure.

Robert had taken off. He'd fought to the last bell, but once he'd been defeated, he faced up to his undoing. Despite his low reserves of willpower, he had made a courageous decision: He would put five thousand miles between himself and the dirt that had created this disaster of his lost happiness and his shattered riches.

This departure, which would profoundly influence my life, didn't at first make any difference to me at all. That would come later. A word from me, and Robert would have returned. I did not want to say this word. I knew only too well that, due to the state of our souls and the status of our affairs, continuing our relationship would have made us both miserable. I hoped that his family, when they saw how much distance he had put between us, would reinstate his allowance.

I held my ground. Much later, when I learned of the hardships of his exile, my heart softened. I better understood that I had not made as great a sacrifice as he did in going so far away. Poor Robert! We had suffered enough for each other. He had devoted so much to me, sacrificed his life for me, so that I would be exonerated in my lawsuits. It inspired the same courage in me that he exhibited during the moral and physical torture that he endured in his long voyages.

At first I had thought of forcing myself to write his story here. But on rereading his letters, I realized that it would be better to let him speak for himself.

The first letter I received was postmarked from London.

47

Correspondence

London, 22 May 1852

I do not want to leave Europe without writing to you one last time. This morning, I saw Dover and the coast of France, and I only tore my gaze away when they were no longer in sight. Adieu, my dreams, my joys, my happiness! I've left it all, and here I am between the vast sea and the sky, all alone with my obliteration from the face of the earth. This is the fruit of an irrational love: misery and isolation! Fittingly, my body won't be able to withstand all that the future has in store for me.

When I arrived on board, I found the glass of my traveling case had shattered, as well as the glass over the picture of you. It's a bad sign. Maybe the end is here. I'm sick. I didn't have the strength to endure even crossing the Channel, which only took a few hours. Have mercy, my God, have mercy! I'm already used up. Maybe you'll find that I didn't deserve all this suffering.

I'm waiting here in London for a ship that leaves on 9 June. My passage is reserved.

I wish that you could see in my eyes and on my face the evidence of your destruction. But I will be avenged for your cruelty to me. Someday, this will only be a memory for me, but it will follow you all your life. I will never return, I can feel it, and my predictions are never wrong. Remember, Céleste, that all those people you sacrificed me for look down on you. You'll be alone in your tower, and not one friend will remain with you. You are beautiful now, you are sublime, you have money, you are such a lovely courtesan when you want to be.

But why is no one thinking of me? Mogador! Who knew how to devour, to shred, to walk all over my fate? Mogador! For whom did poor Robert sacrifice everything? It must have been for a very beautiful girl! Robert, who was above all prejudice, who paraded her on his arm in front of all of Paris!

Oh, she was good for me, that Céleste. So much love! Such mercy for my tears! She has avenged herself on this Robert, who had figured out the only way to make her come back to him, by raising her self-esteem and taking her as his mistress! To his last sou.

She didn't have a minute of regret, not a flash of pity. Go, go, Céleste. This is more than infamy, this is monstrosity. You only used me as a means to your ends. Fine. I only made one promise: At least I made you a profit.

Remember, sometimes, that there is a man in this world that you have condemned to a fate worse than death, and that this man only had words of love and forgiveness on his lips. The public will no longer laugh along with him. He will die in misery and despair. Until that day, he is alone, alone with his vanished dreams, without anyone to whom he can say, "I'm suffering because I love her!" He left it all behind when he left Europe. He doesn't even bear his own name because he left it when he departed. Nothing! Nothing! I left without a kiss, without a kind word! During the long nights aboard the ship, my heart's only consolation is the thought of the kisses that you are giving another at just that moment.

Since I met you, I have not had a single thought for any woman but you. This will still be my only thought during this five-month passage. If God wills that I should not arrive at my destination, my body will be thrown into the sea, and I will die holding your face in my heart until my last breath. Look at my picture sometimes; there is kindness there that is mystical and you might say magnetic. You'll see that sometimes a tear falls from my eye, or maybe there will be a smile that I will send you as I die. If the crew falls, then my picture will disintegrate, turn to dust. That's how I will die. Finally, if during the night you hear, "I love you, Céleste. It's still me, me alone and no other," will you listen? If you go to Poinçonnet, examine everything. Each flower will tell you that I think only of you.

Adieu, adieu forever! I no longer have the strength to even write. It's been so long since I've had an hour of decent sleep. Oh, my strength, my strength, don't abandon me yet! Let me get there, so far away! Let me suffer a few more months. It's all I have left, the suffering she causes me, so let me suffer. I love her!

Adieu! I can't go on. I can't see clearly. I'm going to throw myself on my bed, poor bed, so miserable in a dark little room. I'll only leave it to board the ship. In any case, this crossing of la Manche, which was so awful, has finished me off. I need to rest for at least three days.

I'm leaving with a group of emigrants, almost all Irish. Even the captain doesn't know a word of French. There is a boat leaving tomorrow, but I don't have the time or the means to get to Liverpool. The ship on the ninth leaves from London, which is easier.

I intend to have your picture set in a jewelry box when I get to Sydney. I will write to you, if God spares my life. If I find a way to send you a memento en route, via ship, I will. Adieu, one more time. I forgive you because, I repeat, you will see it all one day. You will be alone, all alone, without friends, and I won't be there anymore. Try to put this moment off for later rather than sooner. However rich you could be, whatever ambition you could have, it's all horrifying when you're isolated, looked at with disgust and disdain.

Adieu, adieu, my thoughts are with you, as is all of my sadness.

Robert

I will write tomorrow to your lawyer, M. Picard, to tell him of your interest.

Toss a note to me by post in London, at the same office, Tuesday or Wednesday, to tell me what will be done at court regarding your affairs. Don't tell me anything else, please; I don't want to know. You must understand that I no longer believe in anything and that, consequently, your excuses, your reasons, your tears, and your apologies will only be lies as far as I'm concerned. But I want to know, whenever I receive your note, what happened at your trial last Tuesday.

Southampton, 15 May 1852

I am writing to you from aboard a ship that, in an hour, is going to take me far from you forever. I'm leaving with no illusions or hope. In London, I had a ring made for you, which I sent on M. Godot's ship, as you are the only person in France, the only being, who showed any interest in me. Maybe this interest only comes from the depth of my depression. I have a traveling companion during this four or five months' passage while I relocate to the country where I will isolate my depression and hide my misery, a boy I met in London. He, like me, is looking to forget his past and find a life outside France. The alignment of our circumstances made for an alignment of feeling, and we find ourselves driven by the same thoughts. He gives me some courage, and we hope to stay together.

You were so beautiful and amazing at the races at Champs de Mars. A pedestal like mine is a lovely one to topple, and I don't doubt for a second that someone will pay dearly for being curious about a character like yours. You'll see, on the ring that I sent you from London, the date 15 May, Southampton. That's the day it was all over for me. Not one friendly voice came to say, "I'll think of you! Thank you for having loved me!" I'm dying of sorrow; I'm dying without leaving behind a memory of myself. You said—you repeated ever since we broke up—that you'll get revenge on my entire life, my whole fortune, all of my youth and dreams. Fine. I hope you're happy; I'm gone. I gave you my future, my life, my heart, my tears, my money for your whims, and I left, heartbroken and dry-eyed, without a pound sterling to live on. I paid for my passage all the way to Sydney. I'll stay there just a week, then I'll sail for other, farther islands. I've decided to eliminate my moral depression through physical exertion.

I am no longer part of genteel society, and the immensity of my love, like the immensity of your notoriety, has been paid for with my misery and suffering. This ring that I've sent you will serve, along with my portrait, to increase in value and even pay for your physical upkeep. Be quick about it, because you're not getting any younger. My only revenge, which I will wait for, is that eventually you will look hideous.

Today, as I depart, it's not you, Mogador, who I loved but a dream, a woman whose memory, whose ideal self, is engraved in my heart. A woman without a name, without a past, a woman of my own creation, of my love's creation, who I dreamed up and fashioned as my heart perceived her. She is dead to me forever, and I pray to God for her every day. It's not you I loved; only what is good and noble can be loved, and the woman that I loved, I adored.

Go, go, Céleste; Providence does not forgive you. The more you bet on my ruin, the unluckier you will be, and the more you'll be dismissed. Even Providence will be merciless toward you, just like you were to me. Your life will soon be hell.

As for me, I'm going to build a new life while the bread you eat will be bought with the contempt of others and covered in filth. You were *ungrateful*! You only kissed me to make your lies more believable.

I forgive you for everything, even the lies and ingratitude. Why would you have any respect for me when I was so gutless that I took all your insults?

I forgive you, but God will damn you as a woman without a heart or a soul.

No one will know where I am. If physical strength leaves me, great! God and everyone else will forgive me because I will have suffered in both my heart and my body.

Adieu! Be happy, if money can buy happiness, and don't make your reputation even worse by saying cynical things about me. Remember the shield on your carriage: Forget me not. Pleasantries can become insults when they fall on a man who had wealth, nobility, a future, yet ended up working with his hands for a living.

Robert

Aboard the Chusan, *15 May 1852, 5:00 p.m.*

I left Southampton at two thirty. There was not a passenger, not a sailor, not an algae that didn't have someone to see them off with a kiss. Yet I am alone, alone and pathetic. The whole city was at the port yelling hurrah and wishing us bon voyage.

Steamships chugged alongside us for the first two hours at sea. Each of the passengers was given permission to bring along a family member for a bit, and some brought their mistresses. Each of them departed sorrowfully, but they all had someone to say to them, "Until we see each other again!" Only I was alone. No one. Not even the consolation of having someone from France nearby who could understand me. They all had someone who loved them, who would miss them.

I don't have anyone who loves me, who will miss me.

While I am writing this letter to you, Céleste, you are basking in your triumph. It's an empty triumph, however, because I am not at all shielding myself. I was so happy to see you smile. O, my God! I suffer so much because I am so alone in the world, and I so need love and affection.

The boats that have escorted us are about to turn back. They have nonstop music on board, which touched a nerve, and I cried like a baby. Crazy as I am! I thought, as we left Southampton, that I saw you in each of the women waving their handkerchiefs in the air, but it's not me they were saying goodbye to. Who could love me? Who could miss me?

Here I am for three months between the sea and the sky. This letter won't reach you for a long time. I'll try to send it when we reach the cape. I'll write to you every day, because the thought of you won't leave me alone. You've done me wrong, and you're without pity, but I forgive you. I'm not thinking of returning, and I'll never see you again, so my last word would be to tell you I love you. And even if I could see you again, what good is wanting it? What good is hope? Haven't I given everything, sacrificed everything, for a hope—a misguided hope—for five years? Do you know what despair is? It's a broken heart, it's a shattered dream, it's facing reality. Well, Céleste, that's what I have now. You fooled me for five years, right up to the day you were merciless. Now what do I care about the miserable future?

Oh, I know your mind. You don't even feel sorry for me. I have my family, you say, who will come to my aid. But what you don't know is that when I die, my family will only find out three months later. Besides, I don't want anything. What would be the cost of my sacrifices if I had counted on others? I can only count on me to survive. My depression almost became my strength, and if I reclaim my lost position in society, it will be solely my own doing.

I'm going to get into bed because I'm very tired. Behold the nights that I spend without sleeping. My poor eyes are bright red. As for the rest, what else could I tell you that would move you? You're happy now, you're free. Your memory of me is already fading into the distance. My only happiness will be to write a few lines to you each day, to think of you. Tomorrow, if the sea isn't too bad. I have your picture near me, and I often kiss it.

Tuesday, 19 May 1852

This is the first time since Saturday that I'm able to sit up a little. Until now, the weather hasn't let me rest at all. I'm looking at the African coast. I spent all my time on the bridge, sitting in a corner, night and day, thinking of the past being carried off a little further each day by a gust of wind. The thought of you should be erased from my memory, like the horizons I can no longer see in the wake of the ship.

I ache so badly—not in my body, because those pains are nothing to me, but in my heart. My poor heart is shattered, and it finds no consolation in the affection that it left behind. Why is it that I gave all that I had to a heart that only wreaks destruction and ruin like a bludgeoning mace? All that you love, you destroy. Everything that is good, you hate. Evil is your essence; the more of it there is, the more you smile. When there's nothing more to destroy, you shove your victims away, you sully them, you insult them.

Since Saturday, I have seen only one vessel from afar. It was headed back to France. Will I ever go back? I don't think so; why would I?

On Sunday, you must have gone to Chantilly. Every day my thoughts turn to France, my poor country, where I thought I was loved! Here's my future: travel to Sydney with the dregs of Europe, among the rush of the English and the galley slaves.

The only help I have on board is a short twenty-year-old Polynesian who knows a few words of French. Having been exiled from Hungary due to war, he is going to make a go of it Down Under like me, without hope or a goal. He's been very sick ever since he came aboard.

The rest seem to be a terrifying gang of bandits fleeing England to escape justice. The boat is very bad, even in so-called first class. They say first is the best, and in second, they feed you trash and you eat the leftovers from first with the sailors. There is another Frenchman in first who is making his way out of Rouen to escape bankruptcy. He dresses kind of flashy for someone who worries about his name getting around; I met him in London before we left.

Anyway, I am so badly equipped for the voyage that I feel like I've been dunked in soup the entire time. It doesn't matter, as long as the weather lets me write to you from time to time. I look at your picture and think of you—who I should hate for all the hate you have for me. I search my mind for why you could want revenge on me—me who loves you. Is it my fault that you are who you are? Didn't I do everything to keep you from leaving? Then why treat me so terribly?

There was no place in your heart for mercy. None for me, nothing but hate. What are you getting revenge for? Is it just how you are? You should be happy now. I've become that same kind of atrocious person. I hate everyone because anyone who has money can steal from me, steal what I love, what I adore.

The boat progresses very quickly, and we hope to arrive at the Cape of Good Hope on 20 June. I'll be almost at the halfway point. Until then, sky and sea.

If the winds are good and if we don't have to dock as we cross the Indian Ocean, I'll arrive in Sydney between 1 and 15 August. Two weeks later, I'll find the young man there who I told you about in my last letter.

I drank copiously during my final days in London, not to shore up my resolve but to erase myself and forget. Far from making me forget, the drunkenness made me even more miserable. The more I suffer, the happier you are, because all this hardship comes from you! How far I am from the days when you said you were so proud of me! I raised you up from your lowly status and from the first day, I protected your livelihood! Do you remember when you told me I would hate you one day? This was already your goal. You hid it until the day you announced it, loudly and to everyone. What a future I had! What status at that time! How I shone! And how low I am today, like everyone, like yourself. You scorned this love that was born of my weakness.

I'm leaving off here because my head is too dizzy to write. Tomorrow, if I can, otherwise on the first calm day. I'm so insane that as I left Southampton, I lifted my head and saw you on the pier! It's crazy, but I cannot close my eyes for a second without seeing you. I saw a woman cry as she watched the ship sail away. Come on, I'm nuts. It couldn't have been you. Besides, does anyone love me?

Adieu until tomorrow.

Friday, 21 May 1852

I just spent the worst day and night. The weather was a little calmer this morning, and I'm able to write a few lines. I spent all last night on the bridge, unable to go down for a moment of rest, but this didn't seem all that long to me. The sky was perfectly clear, the stars were shining, and there was a lovely breeze, a warm wind from Africa that would chap your skin.

How happy you must be; you must always have flowers in your house. I love the countryside. Oh, my poor chateau! Poor Poinçonnet! You have roses, and I—who so generously took care of you, who wanted to tell everyone within earshot: I love you!—I am a poor idiot! I was only a toy whose life and money were nothing. My heart still had to be broken, had to be insulted, and yet I easily forgave her for each injury!

What do you want, my God! Yet today I forgive her. And you alone know, my God, what a life she made for me, how I suffered—me, in whom you instilled so much of your heart, so much love, so much beauty. You alone can see where I stumbled, with whom, and where I was and what I saw.

Behold the spoils of five years of love, of limitless devotion. Here are the rewards and thanks for staying with this woman: ruin and being forgotten. My God, why was she different with me than with others? Why? Because I loved her as she could never have hoped to be loved. Because if she didn't love me, she should at least have respected a passion like mine, a passion I'm ashamed of because she only gave me a rotten life.

She should be on her knees all her life thanking me

for a love that she looked down on, for a love that could have forgiven all. What did she do instead? When she had destroyed me inside and out, she let out a burst of fiendish laughter and said to me, "Look here, you poor bastard. I am only—and only want to be—a whore. You don't have to give me anything anymore; I don't have anything else to sell you. I'll come see you when I have time—but mind you, I'm paid very well. I'll only come to revel in my destruction of you and stick around to watch you suffer."

After all that I did for this woman, look at me now. Look at what she was, yet I forgive her. I don't want her to regret her ingratitude toward me too much. God placed at the bottom of each human heart a real rat called remorse, and the day that it arises, you cruelly rip it to shreds for good without missing a beat.

Mind what I'm saying, Céleste. The day is not far off. Don't fool yourself; your life is damned. You'll be led on your knees to someone, you'll ask for his mercy, and you think you'll touch him with the strength of your devotion, as I tried to do. Then you'll be told, "You're only a whore. Your love is poison." He will answer you as you answered me, with insults. You won't even have the consolation that I have now: having offered and given a beautiful love, a true and proper love worthy of any beautiful woman. I spent my entire life, all my strength, all my intelligence, making a respectable and well-thought-of woman of you. I used everything I had, and I ended up with an ingrate who still had all the vices she had before.

No one knows all my physical pain. No one has the slightest idea of my moral suffering. Misery doesn't frighten me, and I will use my rage to stoke this life that you've destroyed. I must not raise myself from my ruin. I can't financially start over from nothing, and besides, I'm already old, and you need many years to build up a fortune. So I only have the bare necessities for living, and my wits will get me whatever else I need.

If the weather doesn't change, we won't get anywhere for months, and only a week has passed. Four months at sea!

I would be so glad to see a flower! When I get to Sydney, it will be the middle of winter, because it is opposite Paris. When it's midnight in Sydney, it will be noon in Paris, and August is in the middle of winter, so by then I'll have been a long time without greenery and flowers. My spinning head says to tell you goodbye. Until tomorrow. I'm not yet strong as a sailor, and the sea is far from beautiful. In order to be happy at all, I have to write to you. This letter may never reach you. Au revoir! Until tomorrow! Tomorrow, I'll have another wrinkle, because I grow older every day. To age without having lived. To age without suffering.

Until tomorrow!

Sunday, 22 May 1852

It's been a week at sea. I spent the best part of the night on the bridge. The wind was calm, and the sky was magnificent. I sang these lovely verses by Musset that I put to music and wanted to send to you from Poinçonnet:

If you don't love me, tell me, cold-hearted girl.

I sang this all night. Everyone was sleeping, and besides, no one would understand what I was saying. Then, at two a.m., I went to bed and slept and had good dreams. I don't know why the memory of you disturbs my sleep. It's even worse when I wake up. And why write to you? It's more out of the pleasure of you than of writing down my complaints. Anyway, what do I have to say to you? Only the truth that I now know, though it will not much affect you. What does it matter to you? For me, it's to plumb the depths of my thoughts, all that my heart holds of both bitterness and love. It's always the same, like a piece of music in my heart in which the same phrase repeats, but the delicious sound has variations for my soul.

I've made a friend aboard. It's a little terrier, a dog that belongs to the captain. It took a liking to me, and I call it Finoche in memory of your little dog. Finoche, the ingrate! She kissed the joy of every day. She was very happy at the chateau.

This is the first day that we can see land, but it's so far off. If I could have a small flower! Poor fool, a flower! But a flower would wilt by tomorrow. That would make me miss it even more.

I suddenly realized that the captain said we're stopping at the islands off Cape Verde today to refill our water supply. I'll drop this letter off somewhere; it should reach you toward the end of June.

I often go to my pen and dip it in acid. I should resign myself to my suffering; then I couldn't hope for anything else. I'd accept my weakness and not pity myself. But sometimes, it's stronger than me, and it escapes. Then everyone disgusts me so much. My reputation is written on their faces. They seem so surprised to see me in their midst!

Sometimes the captain comes to dine, and I can see that he wants to speak French to learn why I am here.

He must think I'm a very unlucky man, or an extremely depressed one. I'm learning English; it's how I stay busy every day. The food is repugnant, and most of the time I only eat hardtack. As for the rest, I am numb to the privations of the body. You'll hardly be able to read me. It's difficult to write with the rocking of the ship.

All right, that's my letter of the day finished. Is it good? In any case, it's always a joy for you. Love, hate, regrets, contempt, memories: All these are held in your hand. It's your triumph, and in the truest and most lasting things, you'll always find the same love, the one you laughed at and mocked. Poor woman! Your laugh is demonic. Beware the day it changes to a cry of rage and hopelessness. Adieu, until tomorrow! It's been twenty-two days since I left Paris. Your last word was an icicle, a full stop, and I left.

May God forgive you!

Monday, 24 May 1852

I've had a migraine since Saturday, like I used to get in Paris. I couldn't see clearly enough to write.

Today I'm feeling better, and I'm taking to my pen while I can. The pain and suffering are my only consolations. But there's no need to be ungrateful to Providence, because the morning was nice.

The same day our ship left, another was headed only as far as the Cape of Good Hope, on which L… took passage. We passed it this morning, close enough to communicate with each other. I told him of London and all that I'd endured and all that I'd gone through for you. He showed me such affection, and we supported each other.

He loudly called to me this morning: "Courage!" and he placed his hand on his heart. I understood. I watched the ship sail off for a long while. I wept when I could no longer see it. Why? The word *courage*. Courage is so difficult when there's no hope, and what we often take for energy is only anguish.

I write these pages to you because I can't stay below decks, so I have to write on the bridge where my large sheets of paper blow around in the wind. I can't stay seated or in my bed below because there are four of us in my cabin and the heat is unbearable.

I hope that we can stop for two or three hours on Cape Verde the day after tomorrow.

Well, that's my day done. The days and nights are very short for you, and you'll see soon enough how quickly they go by. But for me, for whom everything is painful—past, present, and future—the days are so long, the sleepless nights are so sad. And if sleep comes because I'm just that tired, the dreams are even more bitter, because dreams end, and today is like yesterday, and tomorrow will be like today: misery, memories.

Tuesday, 25 May 1852

We are well into the hottest latitudes of Africa. The sea is like a mirror. Not a breeze blows. The ship moves slowly, and we will arrive at the isles of Cape Verde no earlier than Thursday. The heat of the sun is oppressive. It's impossible to go inside the ship, even at night. So I sleep on the bridge, under the beautiful stars that shine no matter what, knowing that they can be seen in Paris just as they are here. I can't write anything today. I can't muster the strength, nor the begging, nor the scorn. My heart hurts, and I'm still broken. Do you want me to kill myself?

Sunday evening, 29 May 1852

It's been four days since we moored at Saint Vincent, an island off Cape Verde, a desolate land, scorched earth! I think it's the saddest of the sad, and to punish me God is showing me misery and depression worse than my own. He wants to try the innocent as well as the guilty to force men to resign themselves. Here the ground is arid, the land a desert. Death has taken a seat at every door. When going from one house to another, you say goodbye as if going on a long voyage. It has quite an effect; these goodbyes can go on forever. This is a naval town. If the poor inhabitants didn't have faith, the streets would be filled with shouting and blasphemy. More than 1,200 people inhabit the town; 700 were taken by yellow fever. It was devastating. In the houses there are still dead people who haven't been removed. The remaining population seems beaten down and desperate. These poor Blacks seem to be carrying their grief like baggage.

My heart hurts because I can do nothing for them except go see the sick and tell them to be brave with words that seem to bring little consolation.

The missionaries do very well in these countries. The converts to Catholicism are going to die under the auspices of the church while smiling at God.

I went to see Lady C..., a great lady, a saint of a woman who is only spoken of with admiration and respect. She has rudely been forgotten in England, where she would have occupied a high rung of society due to her wealth, birth, mind, and health. She's living in the center of a disaster area, seeking out and aiding the afflicted who surround her.

After having spent a considerable fortune in England, her husband was obliged to take flight. He looked for the most isolated place on earth to live in exile. Cape Verde seemed to him a good enough place to bury his regrets and sorrows. His wife followed after forking over all that she possessed to pay off his debts. Poor woman! Her life was one of virtue, of sacrifice, and of enduring and cruel trials. She did not falter for one minute. Her two sons lived nearby; their poverty did not scare them. They both worked at her side. Every evening, they prayed together and were happy.

If in these thousand things created by God—because man cannot bring them forth—there is a story that makes us believe, there is also, when a catastrophe like the plague happens, proof of our powerlessness. This evil cannot be stopped; who sent it to us? Why struggle against fate?

They just found some Negroes to bring the water and coal that we need.

This island is only a rock, not a blade of grass to be found. The wind, the dust, they blind you, and the climate is so hot, so scorching, that if we stay one day more we'll all fall ill.

We are now at sea. The locals came to the port to see us leave, and they raised their arms for a long time as a sign that they would miss us, and adieu!

Each moment for me is a new depression, and when my strength leaves me, I'm afraid of dying early. I'm afraid that your remorse will not be fervent enough. I wish that you would see the suffering written on my face, all the humiliations, all the public shame, all the tortures that overtake me every second of the day. I accept it all, and with each new punishment, I look at your picture, I say your name aloud without hate, without anger, and that this is all for you and by you. This is your work. Revel in it, be proud, be happy. It's a major triumph, and it doesn't even cost you much.

I am going to get a tattoo of your name on my arm tomorrow so it cannot be erased. If ever my heart forgets you, this name, God willing, will always be there to remind me how cruel and wicked you were to me. I'll need it to remind me of all I've sacrificed for you and how you were fully aware of it. However, this was the only thing I was right to hope for. Your love, though I never believed in it, was mercy, even for the poor dog who only got kisses for abuse. You had neither mercy nor gratitude.

Life is over for me. I feel quite good about the fact that I will never climb out of the pit where you threw me. Despite all my bravery, my strength has left me, and on the day it seems clear to me that nothing will lift me back up, since I will only return to France when everything has been set right, if I cannot do that, I will burn up my brain. Yet this idea of suicide doesn't leave me alone for long, and it comes back stronger than ever when my thoughts turn to you, who I wanted to make so lovely and who became so notorious! There is a struggle inside me between hate, love, and disgust for you, who causes every second of my suffering. Which of these emotions will win? When I see myself among all these passengers, all low class, all the dregs of society, treated like them, looking like them, oh! Then I have the fattest tears in my eyes. I remember the times when I thought I was so great, so noble, so proud, and I remember how I sacrificed this pride and nobility, day after day, in trying to raise you to my level. You were dead set on making me come down to yours. I remember one day, on rue Geoffroy-Marie, when you made a confession to me that I did not ask for. You would have given all your blood that day to be able to offer a love worthy of me.

But all that was an act. You'd already looked for a way to act pitiable at my house, and it worked, because I pitied your tears, I believed your apologies. I thought that your past was the cause of your sadness. I thought you had a little heart, that the man who dared love you, who dared proclaim it, that you would thank him and pay him with a lifetime of devotion.

I hope that, as I write these lines to you, your affairs have been finalized for the better and that you're satisfied with the outcome. You blamed me at one time, which was a wound that pierced my heart. You said that I should be ashamed to see you tormented by my mistake. This reproach was outrageous, but I forgive you. You don't want to see clearly, you don't want to comprehend that my love alone made you a success, that now your life is over.

Sunday, 6 June 1857

The day after I left Cape Verde and wrote to you, I fell ill and stayed in bed all week. It was only yesterday that I was able to get up. My head was too heavy to be able to write. I think that I got this illness due to the climate of Cape Verde plus all of the oppressive heat we've had for several days.

We are not even a quarter of the way along our route and I am already tired of it. It's so bad in second class, and there's hardly enough drinking water to live. The captain and the others have been very gracious toward me. He had probably seen how I was suffering, and he suggested yesterday that if I wanted to pay a few extra louis, I could get a big discount on first class, and he'd be happy to do me the favor. I thanked him as best I could and told him that I would finish the journey as I had started so as not to shock anyone. The real reason is that I have two hundred francs remaining, and that has to last until the day I arrive at the mines.

The memory of me has probably been completely erased from your mind! You should breathe easy. If my name has accidentally come up and ruined your fun and laughter, it was likely in an ironic and sarcastic way. You look down on me, the poor idiot who wanted to be loved!

Oh, you will put on a sad face for anyone who comes near, I predict, and Providence will make you pay dearly for the good times, which you sacrificed all your compassion and heart to have. Providence will hit everything that you love, and if ever in your life you beg for someone's affection, they will answer with indifference.

My God! I couldn't harm anyone. Why destroy me this way? I only know how to love, my God! I could never hate.

It's awful to have only contempt for what you once loved—yes, loved!

Look at the life that's left to me now. I'm going to live and die on the other side of the world. I'll never again see anything that I loved, and no one will hold on to a fond memory of me. Did they send you my ring? It's the last thing you'll get from me. If one day you're feeling bad, if one day you have regret and remorse, come. Bring it to me. You can always find me. The past is dead, but you will find a friend who will offer his hand, who will share with you all that he has earned, who will find kind words to console you if you are upset, who will never speak to you of what you did to make him suffer, and who, when everyone else looks down on you, will have pity for your sadness and will forget his own to tend to yours.

The energy that I have today, the drive that I have to earn some money, it's all for you. I would be so glad to give you what is going to cause me great pain. Listen, Céleste, remember what I'm about to say: If you suffer, if you are sick, if at last you want to quit and leave behind that lifestyle, which cannot go one forever, write two words to Sydney. It will take three months for the letter to get to me; I'll depart immediately for England and count the days, day by day. I will wait for you there, and we will return to the Indies. I will never come back to France, and only one thing could bring me back to Europe: to find you.

But all this is madness. What could you need me for? What could I do for you? What draws everyone to you? You can see that my only hope for the future rests on phantoms. I have to accept it to stop myself from having such dreams. The only truth that remains to me is in forgetting the people, the misery, the work. What good is dreaming? What good is hoping? We suffer even as we dream.

All right, this letter is long enough, and I still have twenty days before I seal it. Let's not waste time that is probably better spent in a manner more fun than reading the sentences and commiserations of a madman.

If by accident the personal effects that I left at your place on Poinçonnet haven't been sold yet, my underthings and my wardrobe would make me happy because

I have absolutely nothing. You would be very kind to send me a trunk with all of my things, including the picture of my father.

Fate is so harsh in reneging on the happiness that had been drained away at the beginning of your life! Things that should have been loved and respected are abandoned and unknown; things that should have been disdained and hated are adored.

My neighbors in the next cabin are from Ireland. I hear, though I don't want to, every angry thing they say. I can get them to pause by moving my chair or coughing, but they go right back to it. Their confidence, which will soon enough become recklessness, could cost them dearly if others hear them.

The man might be twenty-eight years old. He's tall and broad-shouldered, but his waist is as small as a woman's. His hair, naturally curly and tossed back, is like a lion's mane. His eyes are deep set, but they shine and have a hard expression that's intimidating. His nose is narrow, his lips strong. There's something diabolical in his demeanor that's repulsive at first sight.

The young girl who's with him and passing as his wife is blonde and fragile as a child. Her eyes are of a blue so sweet that they make her whole personality more interesting. You'd say that they were plucked from a beautiful spring day. When she speaks, her mouth blossoms like a rose, and her breath is perfumed. She doesn't have a shapely woman's body; she's a poor angel cast to the earth to save a great sinner with her love, or to convert a wretch. She folds in on herself like a fallen angel tucks itself under its wings. Thus sheltered beneath the pain that destiny has brought her, she waits with angelic resignation.

Poor creature! Between her life and mine there is a similarity that strikes me, but she is a woman, and her weakness is forgivable.

Yesterday, after having gambled half the night, he came back drunk. She waited on him, and she seemed to have got him to think about what he'd done, because he lost it. She rebuffed each accusation with infinite kindness.

"I'll leave you if you're not happy," she said, "but how is it possible for me to give myself to you right now? Could there be two lovers for life, and when you've put up with what I've put up with, do they break up for being treated badly?"

"Your complaining makes me tired," said this man pointedly. "I'll end up hating you. You seem unhappy, which I don't like. I didn't force you to come, but since you followed me anyway, your life is entangled with mine. You're my companion, my girlfriend."

"Your girlfriend! Never, MacDonnell! Your confidant, despite myself, maybe. If I don't turn you in, it's because there's nothing lower than being a rat. If I loved you, it's because I didn't realize what you were really like. Once I give it, my poor heart doesn't know how to get out. But I want to maintain the purity of my own soul. My fault lies in my love, and my love will be the punishment for my fault. I shove the pain down. Don't insult me, don't lay more blame on me. Let this love that's killing me count for something. My God! If I'd only loved a man with heart! But this guy, in exchange for my sacrifice, what has he given me?"

"Wrap up your speeches," he said sharply. "If you liked your family so much, you wouldn't have left it."

"He calls out my weakness! But I held my family

as if holding it to a light. I loved my father the way a person loves God. His confidence in you doesn't excuse my crime. Now I know that although the money you took from him when we left was enough, I thought that his money, my money, was left to him as a consolation."

"Fine, I'll take you back," cried MacDonnell, beside himself. "I want my freedom too. If I hadn't stolen that money from your old cheapskate of a father, he wouldn't have given it to me, and I wouldn't have bothered with you. If all the women I've loved, and who have loved me, dogged my steps and cramped my style, I would have a harem. You can say to them, 'I love you!' and it's up to them to come and go as they please. I like easy lovers, and I find them everywhere. Before you, I had another, and I'll have another after you, and that's all there is to say."

"You break my heart," whispered the poor woman, "but I'm like moss, I stay where I'm put. If you don't love me anymore, it's better to kill me to set yourself free."

I heard her crying half the night. I promised myself to offer her my help, my protection, the next day, to help her free herself from a man I regarded as an ass. But when I saw her again on the bridge, she was wrapped in the arms of her lover, smiling at him and looking at him with tenderness. Everything was forgotten! She asked him what he was thinking with a sigh.

How can she love this being who is beneath loving? What did he do to deserve this? I learned some things. They said he was a captain of industry living on who knows what, but she is the daughter of a wealthy trader who had raised her, so they say, like a duchess. I believe it. Her manners are charming, her ways refined and genteel. I could not understand her love for a man who must shock her delicate senses at every turn.

Oh, my God! I love you so much, Céleste. Wild nature, arid heart, untamed spirit! Why doesn't she love him? Isn't the soul mysterious? But this woman, as I said, her weakness is her excuse.

And me? Ah! God damned me, and I am the most miserable of men. That's my story.

Sunday, 13 June 1852

I'm ashamed of myself for how little energy I have to fight off my depression. Despair is everything here; all I know how to do is beg, and my heart is in rebellion.

Sunday in St. Vincent on Cape Verde, I went into a wooden church. A good priest said mass for all the poor Negroes. When you feel terrible, prayer does you good. I asked God to end my suffering, I thought of my poor sister who loved me so much, and finally I tried to write down everything I remembered of all the good I had, everything beautiful and honorable in my life. I cried and left the church, ashamed because, no matter what I wanted, my thoughts always returned to you. I could only bring to God memories made unclean by the thought of you and by my love for you, who put all your glory into being a courtesan.

Poor girl! May God have mercy on you! You only value men according to how they take you for being who you are, and you toss aside those who have any other kind of feeling for you. Ah, Céleste! Céleste! For the rest of my life, I'll remember the first letter that I wrote to you. It was after the death of my father, in response to a letter from you, even though I hadn't given you my address. Because I wanted to break up, I had a kind of vision of the future that you wanted to create for me. I answered you, I told you all my hopes for the future, I described my red room to you and my mother's room (which should have been mine). I told you that I thought about you, and about the landscape outside my window, of nature, of the sun, of all the things you couldn't understand, all the things one loves to talk about when one is in love, because it's the only feeling that gets you closer to Divinity, and only it can raise you up and regenerate you. You forgive and forget everything when you have love as an excuse. Anyway, this letter was my first mistake. When I lost my father, I looked for consolation at your side. That was my first public embarrassment. Since then, God has punished me and rewarded you for it. I deserved all that I got, and even now, this letter, in which each word is a plea, is yet another act of cowardice. I would like to be strong enough to forget it all and laugh about it. I would like to not give the bastards the spectacle of my sadness.

I've found a Frenchman among the sailors. I've made a friend.

My poor sailor endured tortures. And yet it is a rather touching story. Poor child! Yesterday as he was telling me, he seemed to be confessing. They made him pay dearly for a moment of weakness. It blew up his life; he became a dead man for a five-franc coin.

As I listened, I thought of all the joy I could have had with this fortune that I'd wasted without doing anyone any good. I'm sorry I'm not rich anymore, and if I ever get rich again, I hope I know enough to use it better. No doubt, he gave me a good lesson, and I benefited from it. My new friend is named Jocelyn Moulin. He's barely twenty, but you'd think he's thirty. He has a melancholy, thoughtful air. I should write: He *had*, because he could be dead at the moment. I write these lines because his breath was rattling when I left his cabin.

Jocelyn's Story

He was educated some, and he endured much more than others who do the work he had to do. He was a child when he lost his father, and his mother, who had a small business, had that ridiculous idea that's in fashion: She raised him as if he were wealthy. The doormen taught their daughters piano, so she wanted her son to become Raphael. She undertook fifteen years of unimaginable hardships and was able to admit him into an apprenticeship with M. C…, one of our painters who is known for his originality and, moreover, has a reputation for low-down greed.

Jocelyn didn't have any particular talent for painting, but he worked and succeeded by putting in more effort than the others. But he was living far below the standard of the other students, who had better-off parents and could treat themselves to the thousand and one delights that Paris tempts you with at every step, and which are so enticing when you're fifteen. He ate his bread dry, drank water, and didn't smoke, which gave him a certain chic among his friends, who had to give their mentor tobacco as a kind of tribute so he didn't have to buy his own. Poor Jocelyn couldn't go to the theater once a month; he turned down all invitations and resisted the temptation with heroic courage.

But one day, the king held a festival of Saint Philippe on the first of May. The apprentices were up in arms— they had to work until noon. They planned to lunch at Romainville, go looking for lilies, then return to the

Champs-Élysées to see the lights and set off fireworks. Jocelyn lived this nightmare for three days. He turned down invitations to go along, and for good reason: It cost five francs a person. He asked his mother for the money, but she responded by showing him the list of expenses she paid every day for him.

"With five francs, I could buy you shoes next month, and if you spend it on nonsense, you'll have to walk barefoot."

Jocelyn agreed, no matter how much he wanted to go to the festival. But his mother had what she called sense enough for both of them. He went back crying like a child, without even thanking her for the new cap that she'd given him for his party.

He resigned himself to this fact, but on entering the atelier, the attacks started up again. The other apprentices listed the entire festival program; they begged Jocelyn; they said he was stingy, miserly, that he was afraid of being punished by his mommy or that he was afraid to crush his new hat.

Just then, the master came back in carrying a bag under his arm. He crossed the atelier without speaking to his students, went into his room, and emptied a sack of silver onto a table so that he could count it. When he heard the jingling of the metal, Jocelyn felt something like a nervous tremor. There was, right there, so close, maybe a thousand francs in hundred-sous coins, that didn't make the painter as happy as one coin would make Jocelyn. You might say a devil on his shoulder was trying to torment him, because the artist counted and recounted his money with a slowness that made plain the pleasure he got from touching it. He left his door open, and Jocelyn watched him the way a man dying of hunger watches the booth of a food seller.

At that moment, the clock, which had been slow to advance that day, chimed noon. All the apprentices got up as one and went into the next room to fetch their jackets and caps.

"It's not noon yet," growled the master under his breath as he got up to check the time on the clock.

Jocelyn couldn't resist. Quick as lightning, he took a five-franc coin from the pile that hadn't yet been counted and ran like a madman. M. C... returned to counting. All the students went out and found Jocelyn in the street, standing motionless as if he were glued to the pavement. The realization of what he'd done had just hit him, and he was about to go back in when the jokes started up again.

"Be careful," they said, "it's going to rain. You'll ruin your little cap."

"I'm going with you," he said, almost in spite of himself.

"Your mommy!" cried the chorus of apprentices.

At the fair, he gave one of the boys his five-franc coin to pay for their entry.

"It's not fake or anything?" said the boy as he tossed it onto the pavement to make sure it sounded like metal.

Jocelyn turned pale as death. He followed the happy gang, but he was shaking. His fun had died, and the smile on his lips expired. It makes you want to say to him, "Have fun, however little money you have. You can regret it in the morning; today is festival day."

He couldn't eat or drink. His conscience fought him all the way. He berated himself for not doing as his mother said. He said to himself that he should have been happy to eat his dry bread, since he had no bread at all now. This fun day out was a miserable day for him, yet he had no idea what was waiting for him. He told himself, I'll sell something. I'll confess everything to my mother, and she'll come to the atelier tomorrow, and I'll pay back the hundred sous. Oh! I would never dare tell her. I'll throw the sous under a piece of furniture and then "find" it.

Jocelyn lived with the master. When he returned to the townhouse, where he slept in the attic, he searched for something to sell, but he only had the bare necessities. His mother brought his things every week and put them away. He would have to tell her and promise not to be angry with her for the tongue lashing she would give him. He wasn't brave enough to go through with this plan. His mother was good and would pay anything to pave the way for her son to become an artist. She had always been very strict and had quashed with finality any fantasies he might have had outside this plan.

That night, he didn't sleep a single minute, and in the morning he went downstairs before anyone else was up. M. C… saw him but didn't say anything. He just set up his easel and sighed loudly, as usual. Jocelyn hoped he hadn't noticed anything, and he breathed more easily.

The students arrived one after another. It was only when the last was at his work that M. C… asked, as paced the room while searching their faces, "Which one of you filched a hundred-sous piece from me yesterday?"

Everyone started to laugh. Jocelyn became white as the paint he was just adding to his palette. His brush fell from his hand, and he stumbled when he went to pick it up. He wanted to say, "It was me," but one rarely acts on a good instinct like this.

M. C… regarded him again. "Maybe I'm wrong; however, I counted it out, and the person who gave it to me counted it in front of me, and the piles were all the same. When I went to roll them up yesterday, I found I was five francs short. It's funny. I thought you'd played a prank on me."

"With money, never!" said a student. "And I don't think any of us would want to steal a hundred sous from you."

"I would have taken the whole bag," said another.

Just then, Jocelyn's mother came in to ask for the key to her son's room. She had a small parcel under her arm, and she seemed very pleased with herself.

"Well," she said to the students, "are you all recovered from your fun yesterday? You were seen messing about on the Champs-Élysées; that was the only place for you. Our neighbor said she'd seen Jocelyn with you, but I know perfectly well he couldn't have been there, since I didn't give him any money. He moped about it a little yesterday, but I've brought him four good cotton shirts, and we'll make up. He'd only have the memory of yesterday's hundred sous today, but these will stay with him."

M. C… observed Jocelyn for a few moments. He became enraged. Jocelyn tried to keep a straight face, and it almost worked, but he messed up his paints and put yellow in sky blue.

"Well, Mother Moulin, he's more skint than you are," said one of the young men with a laugh. "He was at the festival yesterday, but I don't know if he'd come down with something, because he was no fun at all. If we had known, we would have only taken three francs from him, because he didn't eat anything. But we're a bunch of jerks, Mother Moulin, with more stomach than manners. That's why we're always having guts, right, boss?"

"Where did you get the money?" demanded his mother, irate. "Who do you owe?"

"Which of you loaned it to him?" asked M. C....

"No one," all the apprentices answered. "We only had enough for ourselves."

"Maybe it was me," said the painter looking at Jocelyn. "He only had to reach out."

"Oui, master!" answered Jocelyn confidently, pretending to be friendly with M. C.... "I was going to repay you today. I was waiting for my mother."

"And who told you, you horrible creature," M. C... yelled, "that I could or would give it to you? Do you think I don't have enough for you, you ingrate, so you pretend to make a donation to me?"

Some of the apprentices laughed, while others took the whole thing seriously.

"I do not like this way of borrowing," Mr. C... said. "You are too old for these pranks, and I don't know how to take this, which I do not want to take, because your mother is an upstanding woman. From now on, you are no longer one of my students."

His mother begged, but the painter didn't budge. He was setting an example. The mother repaid the five francs, but her son was treated worse than a thief. She forbade him from entering her house. He found himself broke, abandoned, and rejected by everyone.

He set himself up to paint in a garret, and he had begun to earn a living when a laborer who worked with him and was jealous discovered, who knows how, the reason that Jocelyn had been kicked out of M. C...'s. The story spread by word of mouth, but it was no longer a hundred sous but a hundred francs. Few cared about the actual amount. The story was that he stole, which made him crazy, desperate.

In the end, figuring Paris wasn't big enough for him to hide out, he got hired onto a French ship, and then the English boat that's taking us to Australia. There, he's planning to go work in the mines and never return to France unless his mother sends for him.

Jocelyn looks sweet and kind. He's delicate and nervous, and he must have endured a lot during the five years that he considers his time served.

So now yesterday, the second-class passengers complained that their things are being stolen every night. One lost his tobacco, another his brandy. The captain had no patience with them and told them to lock up their things.

A young Englishman, who was well-known to a number of passengers, said to the captain while pointing at Jocelyn, "Hold on, keep an eye on that guy. He stole money from his master. M. C… chased him off, no lie. I learned to paint alongside him."

Jocelyn heard him and, quick as a thought, rebelled against this unfair accusation. He threw himself at his former friend and, taking him by the throat, screamed, "You're lying! I'm going to strangle you!"

Before anyone had time to separate them, Jocelyn had been stabbed twice in the chest. His adversary, feeling he was weaker, had struck at him like a traitor.

"You have no right to call me a thief!" yelled Jocelyn as he fell. "You're a killer!"

An English sailor who was there was as outraged by this awful cowardice as the rest of us. Since there was no way to serve justice besides doing it himself, he decided to avenge the one we took for dead. He grabbed the knife away from the man who had stabbed Jocelyn and threw it onto the deck, saying, "You are a terrible Englishman, you are, and I am going to break your jaw so you learn how a person who has a heart fights."

Boxing is popular in England, so this was like the signal to start a party onboard. Everyone arranged themselves around the fighters, and the two champs set themselves facing each other, eyes fixed, teeth grinding, fists clenched. Jocelyn's former friend couldn't back out or escape; the circle had closed around him like a human fence ready to keep him in at the first sign of escape. He wanted to find a way out of the situation, but he'd made his case too well.

His opponent had meter-wide shoulders, and he hit the painter in the chest so brutally that it sounded like a blacksmith hitting an anvil. Each blow made a flat sound and brought a roar from the painter's throat, a yell, a plea. He fell onto the bridge, writhed for a second at our feet, then became still as death. Blood dribbled from his mouth, nose, and eyes. It was a terrifying spectacle. I'm a man, and I became faint, while the women clapped for the victor.

The victim was carried to his cabin. We thought all his teeth were broken and sticking out. Even more amazing, a whole bunch of stolen items from other cabins were found—anything that couldn't be eaten. It seemed that he'd wanted to deflect suspicion.

I made a gift of a bottle of brandy to the sailor who had defended Jocelyn, because the poor boy couldn't thank him himself. Jocelyn knew, though, who the thief was. This made me smile, a feeble smile that was like a ray of sunshine in winter. It's all over! That was the only human being I chatted with on these long nights. And now he's dead!

I wanted to say a last goodbye to him, so I couldn't go to bed. The funeral rite was usually done at the break of day so that the sad scene wouldn't upset the passengers. I had counted too much on my stamina, and my already sad soul was done for.

I want to give you an idea of a burial at sea, but I'm a poor storyteller. I try too hard, and I don't always know how to convey the emotions in my heart.

Four bare-headed sailors carried a sack on a gurney. A fifth opened one of the ship's hatches and placed the sack in it. After a few words pronounced in a low voice, he went to eject the sack, but the hatch wasn't closed fast enough to throw Jocelyn's body far. He rolled alongside the ship's flank, and the cannonball that was supposed to make him sink knocked against the hull as if asking to come back aboard the boat. The noise was like the echo of a cannon, and it depressed me. The same fate could be coming for me!

I suffered body and soul; what is one man more or less in the world? On land, he at least leaves a memory of his passing, his name engraved on a stone that proves he was here. Out here, everyone disappears without a shadow of regret.

※

I still had the captain's dog, but he rarely came to see me. The dining in first class is better than second, that's the reason.

I tried to learn English, but the days are short. There's a five-hour difference between Paris and here. When it's nearly eight in the evening, it's twelve thirty or one in the morning. We're reaching countries where it's fully winter, and as a result I'm no longer suffering through the heat that made me so sick for several days. I spend all my nights on the bridge watching the beautiful stars that seem as lovely and as grand as France. I watch the long wake left behind the ship, a wake that takes me farther from all that I love, which I'll never see again. Sometimes the tunes that you used to sing come back to my lips. Then I fall into an ecstatic state; my heart flies back to Berry, to every corner of it, to every place where I left behind a memory. I dream of my beautiful chestnut trees, I dream of flowers, I dream of happiness, love, kisses, and I always wake up singing that song that reminds me of you, singing it to myself, my eyes full of tears. Tears! Always tears! And for who? For what? Lost illusions! Why do you have them? Could you have them? Why love someone who can't be loved? Could you hope otherwise? Stop complaining, Robert, and if you cannot endure it, have the courage to kill yourself.

Thursday, 17 June 1852

Every day I promise myself to end this confession, which is only a fun little topic for you. I promise myself not to start again tomorrow, and every day my heart, being stronger than my willpower, makes me pick up the pen despite myself. And what for? Always the same old song, always the same old tune. What can I talk about that's not in the past? Haven't I said it all to you a thousand times? This heart will always be the same. Oui, Céleste, I would still be glad to prove to you that you are my only happiness. If I could come into money again, if I could dedicate myself to working for it, I would draw on this energy in the sole hope that's left to me: that soon you'll come to your senses, that soon everyone will abandon you at once, and that on this day, I could exact my vengeance. I would come offer you all that I'd earned, and this revenge would be harsher for you than any other could possibly be, if you have even a little heart left. This revenge would be a word of forgiveness. I will try once again to share a happiness with you that maybe in the end you'll be able to appreciate, when you are at last unable to live inside your illusions, with all the prestige that surrounds you today.

You are still my only goal. I'll come ashore with this thought, and I will patiently take up this miner's life that I'm about to begin. If the time imprinted on my face leaves the marks of its passage, I want you to also be able to read the traces of sincere work performed to secure your future.

Friday, 18 June 1852

I looked for happiness! Isn't that a law of nature? I was young, rich, and brilliant, and I believed that I'd meet a woman equally loving and passionate. Much later, I thought she could never discard a man who had sacrificed everything for her. I was wrong. I was discarded, and it was probably my own fault. I was disagreeable, I was too loving, too devoted, too strict. Unhappiness struck me like a lightning bolt, and after having been the accuser for so long, I now resign myself. I absolve you of all that I think you have to complain about when it comes to me. I was not clever enough to hang on to you, and I was cruelly punished for my clumsiness. All I know how to do is love. How can you think of yourself when you're a lover? And so I was a slave when I should have been a tyrant.

I don't understand how I'm still alive having suffered so much and endured so much sadness! You should never get into a relationship when you know it'll fall apart one day. My heart is under attack by the wildest and craziest ideas. It gives in to the latter, whether it's hope or despair. Now the hope that I might cause you to someday feel painful regret eases my own pain. That's the only revenge my heart desires.

Sunday, 20 June 1852

The final blow I was waiting for has come. My heart and soul haven't suffered enough. I'm ill as a result of this wound I got in Spain. There's a doctor on board, and I saw him two days ago. I have to have an operation. I'm going to wait until the Cape of Good Hope. I'll go to the military hospital to see the head doctor, and I'll leave afterward. When I say "leave," I mean to say I'll kill myself to end a life where I have no attachments. I'm lost forever, but you'll at last know that I lived, that I suffered, in a corner of the world. The day you learn that I've died, that it's the end and there's no going back, would you spare a thought for me? On that day, will you turn down a dinner, a party, a song for me? I don't think so, but my last word for you will always be a good word, and a pardon.

Don't blame me for these sometimes harsh letters. Look carefully, and at the bottom you'll always find a love that you won't recognize at all. Forgive me my complaints. Forgive me all that I did and said that caused you pain. Just remember my tears, if they could sometimes move you. What I would give for a flower to send you along with this letter! But I haven't seen or touched one since the bouquet I sent you with my last thought as I left Paris. You haven't found a single kind word to write me since London!

Friday, 25 June 1852

I arrived at nine o'clock, and I'll leave again tomorrow. I can't even consider healing up before I get to Sydney. Meanwhile, I've an inexplicable happiness here. The most beautiful camellias and geraniums bloom in the fields. This tropical climate does me good!

I sent you a heliotrope flower that I picked for you. Will you make a little display for this souvenir when it reaches you from the other end of the world?

All right, I'll post my letter in a second. Be happy and think of me sometimes, of a life that is no longer only a sad memory.

Aboard the Chusan, *20 July 1852*

I had to hurry to close my letter at the Cape of Good Hope, since I wanted it to go out on a boat that set sail on 28 June. You should have received it, along with a flower that I picked at the foot of a mountain while I thought of you. Time passed; it soon catches up with me at the other end of the world.

Two terrible weeks have gone by. Everything was broken, masts and sails. We thought we'd gotten lost, but finally, just this morning, the weather calmed down, and I hoped to put into port.

During the stormy nights, I only had your picture

for comfort. Second-class passengers, who are all the lowest-class people from England, spent the night drinking gin and brandy. There were fights and hurled insults between the drunkards who were bedded down at random in every corner.

Finally I'm not miserable anymore, however big the storm was, but it was so hard for me, with my delicate senses and instincts, to find peace among the filth. I don't even have shoes anymore. The water came up on all sides of what passes for my bed, and I stayed there, wrapped in my blanket all day, trying to keep out the cold, which lingers even now. We're in the middle of winter. For food, I have filthy pork that smells bad, a biscuit made moldy by the sea air, and a liter of water per day, which is more for drinking than washing up. That's the stuff of my life, and still I'm not in Australia, but the future doesn't frighten me. Work will distract me.

Two weeks from today, I'll be in Sydney. I've counted up the jewelry that I have, and I'll sell it there. I'll buy all the tools I need for the mines and head out at once. This letter, therefore, will be the last you received from me. Once I'm underground, busy earning a living, I won't have time for relationships so far from Sydney.

Courage will not leave me, and if God grants me the strength, I hope when I get there to still have enough money to put right all the foolishness that you have to undergo now, and I hope that my misery and work will still serve to secure your future against need. This is my hope, at present.

Sunday, 25 July 1852

It is really time for this voyage to end, because I am used

up and terribly tired. My nights pass almost sleeplessly, or I sleepwalk, with sad and depressing dreams. Your face and the memory of you come together at the head of my bed and seem to take pleasure in torturing me, of reminding me of each moment of my life with you, one by one—each of your contemptuous words, each of your contemptuous deeds. I constantly see your face laughing at my misery, and I am convinced that you only regret one thing: that all of Paris isn't able to see the degree of degradation that you've caused me. Then your triumph would be complete. I was so loved and surrounded by friends; what is left to me now? Nothing! No one! Isolated, forgotten, exiled! Little by little, this sickness is going to kill me. I'll never again see those I loved. The whole world separates me from the memories of my life and my childhood. Oh! My mother! My mother!

Tuesday, 27 July 1852

In two days, we'll reach the first Australian port, Port Phillip. They've set up major mines near there, and almost all the passengers will disembark there. On the other hand, since the captain thinks that all the sailors will run off to the mines, which has happened to most ships, so that he'll not have enough crew to reach the final destination in Sydney, the ship will stay three miles offshore. Boats will be sent out with passengers and goods, and we'll head for Sydney straightaway without putting in at Port Phillip. I hope that we'll be in Sydney ten days from now. God willing! Because I can't take any more.

We're in winter, which is a good season for arriving at the mines. The earth is easier to work, and the snakes—which are numerous and dangerous—are not active. In the summer it's almost impossible to work because of them. As for the rest of the creatures, like tigers and jackals, they're afraid of humans. They only defend themselves when attacked.

I hope to make a friend in Sydney and go together to the mines. That's a must in case we need to defend ourselves. The challenge for me will be in finding someone who's not a thief or a murderer. It's very sad and boring to have sleep with one eye open and always have your pistol under your pillow. The Australian population must be truly terrible, judging by who's on board this ship, who must be the better class of people. If I had enough money to buy myself a tent, I would be much happier, and I have no doubt that with enough courage, I would pass the days happily. Every evening, as I go into my tent, my greatest joy will be to write my thoughts and deeds in my journal for you. Anytime I find a way, I'll send them to you.

The mines where I'm planning to go are near a village named Bathurst, a hundred miles from Sydney, in the interior. However, if on arriving in Sydney I hear that there's been a new discovery, which is very possible, I'd prefer to go to the new site. There's more chance of success, since there are fewer people and less competition.

Yesterday I found a little box that had been packed in my luggage, one you gave me two years ago. That made me happy. All my wealth is in your picture, your hairpin, this box, and four letters from you; these are the only things I'll keep. May your letters not be lies. I've reread them almost every day. Your picture is still with me; the sea air faded it a little, but I hope that it will live on with me. That would be nice.

Wednesday, 28 July 1852

Since yesterday we've sailed quickly and are fast approaching Port Phillip. I think that tomorrow we'll be close enough to let all the people off who are going to the mines. It's a unique sight for everyone else, these people who are going to seek their fortunes. They're extremely excited to get there, and for the past two or three days, the debauchery has doubled. They've been dead drunk nonstop.

What's sad is that the few belongings I brought with me are completely ruined, so I'm stripped of everything, so to speak. Everything is very expensive in Australia. I have to cover my own costs.

The day when the remorse hits you, the day when you at last become disgusted with everything around you, come to me. You'll find forgiveness in my heart and a kiss on my lips that will erase the past.

Thursday, 29 July 1852

What a horrible journey I've just had. I was about to end my letter to you yesterday, Wednesday, and I'd been in bed for two hours when we were taken to the bridge. A typhoon had slammed into the ship on both sides. We could only see the sky above; the boat was below the crests of the waves. A cry of despair rose among us.

A sailor fell from the high mast right in front of my eyes and rolled into the sea. The ship, pushed by a ferocious wind, sent us along at a speed I didn't know it could do. One mast broke. In the midst of all this confusion, two officers on board, followed by four sailors, used a hatchet to cut the ropes of a small lifeboat. They lowered it, in spite of the captain, to search for the lost man, poor bastard. We couldn't stay on our feet. The ship let out fourteen knots. The lifeboat was far off; we lost sight of it for two hours. The passengers wailed, desperate to stop the ship to wait for these poor souls. I sided with the captain, who hesitated. As great as the danger was, could we abandon them? He ordered the maneuver and turned the ship on a knife's edge to save us body and soul.

I'm writing to you with this in mind. During that terrible typhoon, the memory of you never left me. At last we could see the lifeboat, which balanced atop the gray waves. The men were rowing flat-out, broken by fatigue. Their search had been in vain. The sailor was lost.

All the passengers set to pulling the ropes. Lieutenant Bencraf and the crew who had accompanied him fell unconscious onto the bridge. In an attempt to save the life of their unfortunate mate, they had done all it was humanly possible to do. I gave this young, brave officer my tie pin—you know, the one with the wreath of pearls, diamonds, and rubies. I wanted to be able to give him the cross. For three days we were all under a sad cloud caused by the loss of this man.

We can see the coast of Australia. The first thing it offers to our eyes is a ship smashed on a rock. We have its pilot on board. God wants me to arrive only to submit me to the harshest tests. Death was too good for me. As he wills it, so be it!

48

My Legal Education

I DON'T THINK I'M READING them wrong; these letters from Robert were lovely and touching. When I reread them now, I feel happy. I feel proud of having inspired such a good man, so brave in his hardship, so tender and true. But then my heart is too confused to know what it wants and whether it could love or hate him. Besides, this correspondence only came to me in fragments—sometimes a single letter, sometimes a stack of letters, according to when the ships arrived. The burst of energy they gave me only ever lasted a day. The letters where Robert told me that he had left England were the only ones that reached me quickly.

My situation was awful. I could feel depression coming on, which for me means death.

When one has occupied a high social position, like Robert, when you're noble and rich, you can imagine your ruin without despair. The fall from on high causes vertigo, but for certain high-class types, the vertigo is not without its charms. It's a novel feeling. You hope to climb back out of it. You watch baffled as, in this high-class world, you find people willing to forget the past, who offer their influence, their protection, their hand to help you back up, especially when you have one of the best names in France and rich and powerful parents.

But for a poor creature like me, who has no family or protection, and with a past like mine, when ruin comes, it is definitive. I knew it. I was never under any illusions about the future for courtesans. Knowing with what contempt people spoke of my kind, I promised myself to get out before the humiliation of old age. I always told myself that if, at age thirty, I didn't have a way to live independently, I would take refuge in suicide. I didn't feel I had the courage to bear this poignant sadness that comes with the lie of false luxury within which I'd been living. I didn't have the courage to exhaust myself in the contempt and humiliation that are the flip side of the coin that interested men show to young, beautiful women who they want to see fall. I would never have accepted the trade-offs for this notoriety. I have my pride, misplaced though it may be, which has kept me from doing myself real harm.

I have to try or die. That may have been the only advantage I had over Robert right then. Since my fall wasn't as far, my ruin was not as devastating. He was obliged to head for the ends of the earth. Me, I could stay and try to recover my money from my enemies in court.

But that takes courage and experience that I was lacking at the time. What made things even worse was my moral situation. I no longer knew who I was; my mind was a mess. I became an enigma to myself. The false pride that had made me envy the success of fashionable women, those moneylenders of the soul, had been beaten down. What had replaced it was worse than all human suffering: indecision. I didn't know anymore what was good and what was bad. I'd never had more need to keep busy, and I no longer had the energy to do anything.

I remained in a stupor for several days. If this state had persisted (I could never stand being depressed for more than three days), I would have killed myself. What saved me was the sheer amount of my pain and even the complication of my position.

I have such a rage for life inside me, such a drive to exist, that my character has often carried me over obstacles I'd believed were insurmountable. The months that I spent this way are, to my eyes, a real problem. I don't understand how I could have suffered so much sadness, so much exhaustion, so much going on.

As I had foreseen, they seized my apartment on rue Joubert, my carriages on rue de la Chaussée-d'Antin, and my house at Berry, and they denied the promissory note that Robert left me for money I had lent to him. All of these cases were divided up, and I had a trial in every courtroom.

The lightning of my relationship with Robert and his departure had rumbled like thunder in my circles. Bad reputations are like good ones: slow to acquire, but when they reach a certain point, they run on their own.

Everyone came looking for me, so out of necessity I rose a few more rungs on the scale of elegant vice. I continued to live inside this whirlwind, but for a long time I hadn't had the heart for my public persona.

My life became a double lie: a financial lie and a moral lie. People thought I was rich while the ground was crumbling beneath my feet. I was thought to be more perverse than ever while my soul wanted better than the life I had. I was like actors who are happy on stage and so sad in their personal lives, where hardly anyone knows them.

In the end, I had four lawsuits on my hands. My future, and that of my little girl, depended on justice. I saw with terror my wealth and my life being caught up in one of those ruinous trials where the gain doesn't always outweigh the loss. I asked myself: What does a woman like me weigh on the scales of justice? I suffered doubly for the question of my standing and my self-esteem.

My lawyer in Paris, M. Picard, a man of high intelligence and merit, gave me excellent advice. He sent me to M. Desmarest, who was willing to plead my case, or rather my cases. I had a lawyer in Châteauroux, M. Berton-Pourriat, a caring man devoted to the cases he represented. He, by the grace of his vigilance, provided crucial services. All the people I spoke with were welcoming and devoted. No one took up these cases for the glory, and to undertake it during an outbreak of war made me thankful for these sacrifices.

I had always been curious and always loved to look into things that interested me. If at the start of my life I had had one intellectual focus, my life might have been different. I had to explain my rights, I looked into the laws, I listened, I asked questions, I wanted to understand, to know. I learned all the steps that were taken on my behalf.

In my usual way, I asked for explanations of the many people who controlled one thing or another. I made sure the businessmen were working hard and not because one of them, having compromised himself in his zeal for my opponents, was going to be put on trial. I was not slow to understand the mechanisms of the justice system. I familiarized myself with the terminology that at first had caused me so much worry.

I spent my life at that point in the study of bailiffs, lawyers, and judges. For six months you could only find me at the Palais du Justice.

If I became very knowledgeable about law, it was definitely the fault of my antagonists, because as I already told you, they brought this to trial in every court: civil court, commercial court, and criminal court, where I was defamed regarding a maid who had stolen silver from me and about whom I'd had the audacity to file a complaint.

When all my of my trials were underway and I could not take even a little break from my hectic schedule, I became seriously occupied with my theater.

Flattery no longer turned my head. I knew this life wouldn't last long. I wanted to leave the courtesan life before the courtesan life left me. My only prospect for the future was the theater. I clung to it like hope, but my life was devoured. Courtesan, actress, plaintiff—it was more than enough to fill anyone's life. I ran from the courtroom to the salle des pas perdus, and from the salle des pas perdus to Variétés.

There must be a spiraling in certain moral situations that passion attracts like lightning. I was down and disenchanted; I could only see affection and devotion around me.

Around this time, I heard news that brought me great pain. A woman I had known when I lived on rue Geoffroy-Marie came to see me. She told me that

Deligny had been killed in a duel. I remembered how good he had been to me, and I gave her my sincere condolences.

I won my first case in court, over furniture from rue Joubert. This success gave me confidence. In seeing that justice had been served, even for me, a sweet feeling penetrated all the way to my heart. This busy life that had frightened me now had its charms. I was astonished to think of things that had never occurred to me before, or that only showed up as distractions from the whirlwind of my world or the training of my youth.

I was disgusted by the dependence my lifestyle required. As a measure of how far this had burrowed into me, I regretted not having relied on my intelligence as much as I had my beauty.

The trial for the Poinçonnet property was set for August at the court in Châteauroux. My opponents, furious over their first defeat, used extreme tactics, as usual. I had to travel to Poinçonnet. This was very upsetting for me, thanks to the memories that resurfaced with each bend in the road. The trees, the train stations, the shrubbery all spoke to me; I again saw Robert's face.

This sadness quickly grew into regret over our happy past, of so many dreams vanished, of so many illusions destroyed. I was distraught when I got to my house. Someone had started a garden. I had to wait an hour in the courtyard for the irritated warden to authorize me to enter my own house, which he did with little enough graciousness. This put me on edge.

Several days later my opponents came to ransack the house. They went through Robert's most private papers, hoping to find proof that I was only an alibi. I have no idea why there were fine with making a scandal of it, dragging a good name into the muck in the most distasteful way.

These inexcusable maneuvers, which would not be permitted against people who are capable of defending themselves, were evidence of the discombobulation of my enemies. They offended the court and disposed it in my favor. I was defended with such heart by the talented M. Desmarest, who came to enter my plea in Châteauroux.

Robert left behind good memories in Berry, and whenever anyone tossed off an insult about him in front of the audience, the judges and auditors shouted them down.

I stayed at the hotel Promenade to wait for the trial to end. I had the anxiety of someone who was waiting to be condemned to death. Would the house be sold to the highest bidder? Were they going to evict my memory of this place, which always reminded me of Robert's plans for future projects and where I had hoped to die?

Mme. Edouard Suard, the proprietor of the hotel, made all kinds of efforts to calm my worries for two long and dire days. She's a good and honest creature, too strong in her virtue and too fair of mind to fear coming into contact with a low-class woman to give her comfort, to settle her distress. It was not the first time that I appreciated the generosity of her heart. When I came out here for the first time, we alighted at this hotel. After that, Robert often brought me here while he hunted in the forest. Without this friendly and kind person, I would have been left alone, shut up in a room, for days at a time. She would come spend some time with me, or make me come down to the salon with her, a little sanctuary decked out in flowers, handmade crafts, precious antiques that people admired. A life of order, labor, and faith.

I was happy to listen to her good advice and proud that she would even give it to me. Despite my personality and way of life, which distinctly contrasted with my deepest thoughts, I appreciated highly all that was elevated in the homes of other women.

This feeling of devotion that seemed so easy for her to accomplish seemed to me a heavy task to achieve on this earth. The temptation of evil presents itself nonstop and in all forms. On meeting an honest woman, my heart grew, my soul lifted. With kind words and a little perseverance, I could be freed.

Those who were able to work this miracle weren't interested in doing so. Besides, there's always half the world that sins and half that does good. If a mother with a family took in a fallen woman to help instill a pure, simple joy inside herself; to show her that she'd lost her share of paradise in the world; and to lessen her regret through conversion, even if it's late in coming, as long as she is sincere, she will not be any less accepted by God and all who believe in him.

I gave Mme. Edouard a deep appreciation. I held myself at a reserved distance, which people often take for coldness in me, though it's actually fear. I delivered justice to myself, because I didn't think anyone's contempt for me would ever equal the contempt for myself that Robert had inspired in me.

M. Edouard went to the court, and he was the first to give me news of my trial. The two lawyers from Paris, two celebrities of the bar, were present. The meeting was testy. They hoped I would win, but nothing was certain yet because the verdict hadn't been handed down.

M. Edouard Suard was extremely animated, but deep down he had an excellent heart. He'd done business with

Robert, and he held onto the most affectionate memories. Also, outside this wretched trial, he squared up to help me get out of this trouble. He reassured me, and he brought me a little hope.

I wouldn't know the outcome of this trial for three months. The plea had been entered 31 August, but the judgment wasn't made until after the holidays.

It wasn't so miserable having to wait so long, but alas! I was in double trouble. I'd only won this round; my opponents appealed to the imperial court in Bourges.

These first two important victories allowed me to hope. Little by little, calm returned to my heart, and the facts of my past life came back to me with a jolt. I became less constrained with my happiness. I felt more generous toward others and more strict toward myself.

The distance and events that seemed to unite us had put Robert in his true place in my heart. I began to feel terrible for his exile. I hadn't received any letters except those he'd written the day he arrived in port. I waited impatiently for news.

My thoughts were on these distant horizons where he had hidden away his depression and misery. I tearfully reproached myself. I doubted that God would ever pardon me for this depravity.

I thought up a thousand projects of atonement, of devotion, of repentance, that I could promise should Providence help me to accomplish them.

To get to the little house where I lived on avenue de Saint-Cloud, you had to cross a garden enclosed by a fence. The salon was on the ground floor. The fireplace faced the door, which had a window that allowed me to see everyone walking by on the avenue. I could see anyone who rang at the iron fence.

It began to get cold, and I had to light a fire. I sat in front of the fireplace and was mindlessly watching out the window when someone opened the gate without ringing. I let out a loud cry.

It was Richard.

I recognized him immediately, though he'd horribly changed! He said my name. I wanted to sink into the ground. What was he doing here? To throw accusations at me, to throw his wasted life at me, his lost happiness?

When my chambermaid asked if I wanted to let him in, I remained frozen in my chair, not able to find a word in response.

The door was still open, and he said to me in a gentle voice, "Do you not want to see me, Céleste?"

I nodded yes. He came in and, fixing his gaze on me—still full of adoration even through his suffering—he held my hand and said, "Do you not want to kiss me, Céleste?"

"Oh! Oui, but I don't dare. You must hate me."

"I never stopped loving you." He gripped my hands passionately. "Without the memory of you, I would have killed myself! I always hoped to see you again. I was almost always ill. I had a fever constantly.

"However, I'd built up a small fortune. We had, one of my friends and I, a house that we own together. Fire ravaged it. I wept at this bad luck, only because it would put off my return to France and extend the time before I would see you again. I sometimes had news of you from the Frenchmen who came to California. I learned of M. Robert's misfortune. I felt sorry for him and forgave him for all the wrong he'd done me. I didn't know if you'd tried doing that too. Time heals all wounds, lessens hatred. There's only my love for you that time could not change.

"I rebuilt the house in San Francisco. I rented it to a banker, and here I am. I arrived yesterday, and I chased down your address. It does me so much good to see you!"

"It does me so much good to know you don't detest me!"

"I detest you so little," he said, "that if your heart has changed, and if you would accept what I proposed two years ago, I would propose again. But I know perfectly well that's impossible." He smiled sadly.

"My darling Richard, you have a heart of gold. I don't deserve even a glance from your eyes. The harm I've done you has brought me no good, and I'm no happier than you."

"Oui," he said, "I know that M. Robert left the country, and that all you have left is what I gave you. If you have enemies, you know that you can always count on me."

I looked at him, horrified. The wave of emotion and pleasure that his visit had given me had caused me to forget my call time at the theater.

We were restaging a piece called *Taconnet* for the debut of Frédérick Lemaître. To be honest, the great artist was not patient. Richard drove me there, only leaving me when we reached the door of Variétés and of course getting permission to see me again.

I had one less weight on my heart. His return had done me good. However, it struck me that his presence at my house was an affront to the memory of Robert. I was sorry I'd given him permission to see me again, and I promised to take it back the next time I saw him.

49

Theater Variétés

I prepared myself to re-enter Paris society. The season was becoming too rigorous to leave it to chance, and there was no longer any reason to stay away from my house.

I worked hard at my theater, but it was still less than satisfying. Some of the women were backstabbers, and some directors and playwrights only cast me as maids, beggars, and dancers. I didn't have the spleen, nor the height, nor the body type for those roles. I was miserable, because it was always my fault.

I was very unhappy with the role I'd been given in the most recent show. The role was Queen of the Bacchanal, the kind of character everyone wanted to play. It only required being well made, since the costume was the same as what the living tableaux wore. This was not what I'd been promised, and I made it known to the director that if he didn't want to give me a role that I could work with, I'd quit. The playwrights were spoken to, and they ended up giving me (after someone else turned it down) the role of Crystal Palace in the *Revue of 1852*.

I was struggling to fit into a role that you'd think suited me. A new dance, the Imperiale, came on the scene, and I was asked to dance it with Page. I accepted, though for a while I'd wanted to end once and for all choreography being shoehorned into each and every show whether it made sense or not.

I liked anyone who had talent. I defended my favorites with a fervor that always left me at the top of the game whenever there was a discussion.

It goes without saying that I was a fan of the great tragic actress, the magical talent, sublime, undeniable. She found her detractors among those jealous, mediocre actresses with nothing to animate them but their constant shit-talking and having only a pretty face to their name. They'll stone her, physically or morally. Feminine jealousy always finds its target.

One day, during a rehearsal for the revue, a pretty little Jewish girl spoke very disrespectfully of Rachel, that true queen of the theater scene. I could not attempt to come to the defense of someone who was not there to answer for herself, since I only knew her from seeing her onstage and having applauded her like everyone else. I remember just crying, quivering, and blanching more than anyone else when I heard her.

After watching her in *Phaedra*, I went back to my place feeling a fever coming on. I was delirious with enthusiasm. All night I heard the vibrant, plaintive, sonorous voice of the actress ringing in my ears. No ancient statue had ever seemed to me as beautiful as

Rachel! This concentrated power, this smile full of hate and disgust, giving the full range of rage or love—all of this was new to me. It seemed supernatural. During the show, my soul was suspended in the pleats of the tunic in which the great actress draped herself so well. Everything around me disappeared; I heard and saw nothing but her. I remained under her spell for a long time, which made me adore the Théâtre-Français.

I will say that, like all powerful people, Rachel was attacked. As for me, who was seriously inspired by her genius, I rebelled whenever someone found her less than perfect.

"She is proud, impertinent, haughty," said the Jewish girl on the day in question about *Andromache*. "I knew her when she was broke; I loaned her everything, including my dresses, when she was singing in the streets. Now she doesn't even say hello to me."

This ingratitude seemed completely out of character for Rachel. I knew, because the secrets of her life came out in public the same way the secrets of great men do. I knew that she was generous to a fault, indifferent to the heights where her genius had raised her. Far from blushing over her wretched past, she spoke of it herself. She surrounded herself with people who had known her when she was a child. So I knocked my colleague down a peg by asserting that she was making up knowing Rachel, and especially that she'd loaned her dresses. She swore to all the gods it was true. I believed her less than ever and promised myself to find out the truth.

You couldn't just be Mlle. Rachel's guest anytime, when she was seeing guests at all, because the curious and the rude surrounded her little building on rue Trudon. I was not invited, but I walked toward her place as I left the theater, having decided to see for myself.

When I got there, the concierge, who was ensconced in a pretty little nook to the right of the door, motioned for me to sit in a beautiful easy chair à la Voltaire and asked me to look at the paintings and *objets* while he went to see if Mlle. Rachel was available. I was sorry to have come. What was I going to say? How was I going to come across? What excuse was I going to come up with for my visit? The truth was the last thing I wanted to tell her.

I was lost in my thoughts when a uniformed servant came in, not the one who had gone off to announce me. The new one came to take me in at his leisure. Then, after having examined me for several seconds, as if his response depended on how he found me, he said, "Madame is in her office; she's not seeing anyone today. Come back Thursday at two o'clock. Madame will see you then. If what you have to say is urgent, write to her."

I had been afraid of an unequivocal dismissal. My heart relaxed. I became as happy at the idea of seeing her and chatting for even a few seconds with this sublime, to my eyes, woman as an astronomer would be to stroll among the stars. I dined that night at the house of someone who had a lovely garden, and I was allowed to pick a bouquet. He arranged such beautiful, rare flowers that I had the bouquet sent to Mlle. Rachel with a letter where I thanked her again for agreeing to see me.

I still hadn't come up with an excuse, but one found me. Thursday morning, at eleven o'clock, an artist, the father of a family who was holding a benefit at Variétés the following week, came to offer me tickets. Well, he really wanted me to buy them from him. I took two box seats facing the proscenium and sent them off to Mlle. Rachel.

I spent two hours getting ready. I was thrilled and nervous at the same time.

I'd never had a royal audience, but if I had the chance, I'm not sure it would be more nerve-racking than when the servant said to me, "Well, mademoiselle. Madame is ill, but she will see you anyway."

He stepped in front of me to show me the way, and we went up a narrow, winding staircase. When we reached the second floor, he opened the door and announced me.

"Have her come in," answered the voice that had made me sit up straight so many times.

The room I entered was long and wide and simply furnished. The walls were covered in Persian tapestries; the rugs were from Smyrna. What struck me, due to its oddity, was Rachel's outfit.

She was lying in a bed that faced the door. Her breasts were half out. She wore, over a sheer linen nightgown, a green velour jacket with gold buttons and Grecian sleeves. Around her head she had wound, with unmatched artistry, an Algerian scarf in bright colors. From each side of this kind of Jewish turban fell the fringed ends of this scarf. Her black hair escaped in places in careful little curls.

In one second, she made me believe in all the beauty of the Israelites described in the histories of the saints and so well illustrated by Horace Vernet. I was both speechless and ashamed. I had long been told that I looked like Rachel. At this moment, the resemblance seemed impossible and insulting to her. She also seemed to be looking for this resemblance, because she examined me for several seconds in silence.

"Sit down," she said, gesturing with her alabaster-white hand toward the overstuffed chair placed near her bed.

"You've led me to believe you have something to tell me. What can I do for you?"

"My God, madame," I said, a little reassured by the entirely gracious way she spoke these words. "Even this very morning I was looking for an excuse that you would consider at least believable, and one came to me today. I thought I should tell you. They say that I have good luck, but I don't want to get off topic.

"What brought me to your door the first time was an immense desire to see you up close and to express my gratitude for all the deep emotions that your talent has evoked in me. This seems like being overly curious, it's true, but it comes from the heart, and I hope you'll forgive me."

Mlle. Rachel held my hand and said, "Sit nearer to me. I must speak little and quietly. I have a cold, and my throat is sore. You are entirely forgiven; the pleasure that you say you felt is shared. I'm always glad to learn that even one person feels what I'm feeling."

At this moment one of her sisters came in holding a roll of paper in her had. She came, I think, to report something. (I don't know if this was Dinah or Rebecca.) She was small and delicate as a child.

"Leave us," Mlle. Rachel said to her with a kiss on her forehead. "You can come back in half an hour."

She left, looking at me as if to undress me with her eyes. Evidently, she knew who I was and was also looking for the famous resemblance.

When she'd closed the door, Mlle. Rachel said with a smile, "And could I ask you, without prying, what the excuse is this morning?"

"A show to benefit a brave boy who asked me to buy tickets."

"It was a good idea to come up with another motive to your visit. I am bombarded by requests morning to night, and sometimes from night to morning," she said with a laugh. "If I acted in every benefit show every time I'm asked, I'd spend my life in every theater but my own. I take a cut, and I refuse without pity to pay for my seat, but it's not the same for boxes, and I put myself at your mercy. How many do you want to give me?"

"One, unless you want to turn me down."

"One is not enough. You'll bring me another for my mother."

"I'd prefer to accompany you myself if you'll allow it."

"What a big heart," she said, taking my hand for the second time.

I went back Saturday. She was in her salon on the first floor, to the left as you walked in. There was a garden of espaliered ivy, a divan upholstered in tapestry with Kashmiri designs, and as you walked around the room to the right, an armoire with glass doors that held a thousand curios. I hadn't seen Mlle. Rachel's suite before. She was now seated in a large chair with her back to the window. Above her head, in an oval frame, hung the portrait of a child. This was her eldest son, a gorgeous little boy whose gaze, as intelligent as his mother's, seemed to follow you everywhere.

"My son is handsome, non?" she said as she stood. "He is a true treasure. How are you?"

"Wonderful, and you? Better, I hope, since I see you're up and around."

"I'm doing quite well. Did you bring me my box seats?"

I gave them to her. She waved me toward a seat with her hand, looked at the ticket for a few minutes, and seemed to completely forget about me. Her outfit was somber that day and added to her air of sadness. She wore an old black moiré silk dress with wide pleats around the waist. Over it was a black jacket with matching laces to close it; a collar and cuffs imprisoned her neck and wrists. Her hair was arranged in smooth braids, and only one little curl in the middle of her forehead betrayed the tamed waves. For a moment, she seemed on the verge of a great bother as she roamed the world of her thoughts.

"Excuse me," she said as I stood, "I'm consumed by worry. I'm about to turn down a role. They'll force me to play it, but I'll leave the theater. I could always say I'm sick. Ah! Hold on," she said, changing her tone. "This is for the charity box seats."

I took my leave and, as she didn't ask me to visit again, I left rather sadly. The heightened charm she possessed had worked on me like it worked on all who came near her. You love it when you see it; you crave it when she speaks to you.

Five days later was the show for my colleague M.... She came to Variétés. Between two acts, he wanted to thank her, and I was with him.

That evening, she was as beautiful as a star. She was radiant, and her eyes shone with the light of life and kindness. This gave her face an entirely different cast. Her mouth was smiling, her voice sweet. There was only one opinion moving from mouth to mouth; everyone said, "How beautiful Rachel is tonight!"

"Come see me," she said just as I was about to leave. I thanked her again with a look that expressed all my gratitude to her, but I didn't want to overstep. I waited two weeks before going back to rue Trudon.

When I saw her again, I spoke to her of this woman who had said she knew her well. Mlle. Rachel assured me she'd never seen her, and I believed her.

I laughed so hard and for so long at my colleague that she quit Variétés.

In all, I visited Mlle. Rachel seven or eight times. I found her charming but a little prone to exaggeration, which she's allowed.

They said that her variety of personalities stemmed from an illness, a nervousness, independent of her will. She suffered from this unpredictability that left her only long enough to plan a project for the future. What she liked one day she didn't the next. She built up idols only to break them for fun.

She was a siren, an enchantress, that you loved despite yourself. She could not be forgotten when you knew her during her good times. She was affectionate, simple, generous, indulgent. When nothing irritated her, her manners were impeccable, like a duchess, it's said. But when she was irked, the storm of her personality was as terrible as the good times were calm.

I thought her instructive. She was a wonderful storyteller and knew how to listen with infinite patience.

A new concern came to add to my theatrical troubles, and I went several weeks without seeing her. I didn't dare go back, but I thought—and still think—of her often.

50

A Star

I RARELY SAW RICHARD. I was at rehearsal almost every day. One evening, he requested that I await his arrival. The next day, he arrived at the appointed hour. I was struck by how down he was.

"I came to say goodbye," he said. "I wasn't honest with you, so as not to worry you about my leaving. The San Francisco fire left me with nothing."

"What are you going to do? My God!"

"There's nothing to do; it's done. I hired on yesterday as a lowly soldier in the foreign legion, and I'm about to join my regiment in Africa."

I had no standing to fight his decision. He didn't seem like a desperate man, but rather like a man who wants to regain his vitality by training like he had in his youth. The last thing he said to me was a wish for my continued happiness.

My trials were on hiatus. Things moved with demoralizing slowness, which resurrected all my worst fears.

I was invited from all sides to dinners, to balls. I went. I had people over, but it was less for fun than distraction, to give my good friends a change of scenery and my depression a reprieve.

I lived at the theater five hours a day. I had already acted in a show by the creators of the revue, but I only knew them a little. They were two lovely men; one was a real mockingbird. He did marvelous impressions of all the actors in Paris. One day, he did the enchanting vocal organ of Pelletier, the actor from Funambules, in the hallway, followed by the voice of Laurent of Ambigu. The other creator, M. D…, was a man of heart and honor. He was very reserved with the women of the theater, even cold toward them. He only made an exception for me, and I took this as a gesture of friendship. I of course needed this support more than other women, which put me in the middle of a heated war of gossip and praise.

B…, for example, is the most original woman I've ever met in my life. She screams her head off. Every year, she wants to be two years younger. She only speaks of her well-mannered ways, and she is jealous of the emcee. Otherwise, she is a fine person as soon as she leaves the stage.

Ozy, with her sweet voice and pretty mouth, didn't even spare her inner circle. Once, she left the theater dressed to the nines, and M. C…, the director, asked where she was going. She answered, "Mother Mary! I'm going where you've condemned me to go, Mogador's, since you make me work with her."

He said, "But I don't think there's anything in your contract about you going to her house?"

She surely made me a thousand friends that day. She ran her world like a noblewoman.

M. C… had as his accountant the strangest man you could imagine. He was fat, short, and gray all over. It was said he was an Armenian Jew, but it was difficult to know where he was from because he spoke five or six languages badly. His administrative procedure was to not pay anyone. When you asked him for money or costumes, he answered in German. If you insisted, he spoke Hebrew.

He had, along with the theater's concierge, a story that kept us amused for a week. The concierge brought him a request.

"Thirty sous, more or less," said the accountant looking at his invoice. "To do what, more or less?"

"Monsieur," said the concierge timidly, "it's for cats."

"To do what with the cats?"

"Well, monsieur, to eat the mice that, without the cats, would eat the sets."

"Well!" answered the Armenian, red with rage, "if the cats eat the mice, they don't need anything else. If they don't eat the mice, then we don't need the cats."

And he refused to pay.

These bizarre incidents were very funny, but they kept the artists broke. I had three costumes in the revue. I had to buy all three because if I didn't, I figured he'd make me dress like a Turk.

I still owe my having met one of the most brilliant stars to shine over Paris, an indispensable ornament to the city's glory, to my admission to Variétés. As small as its footprint in the capital was, we were always proud to shine there, if only for a dress or a hat. But the person I'm talking about did not need dresses from Camille or hats from Laure. For luxurious decoration, she had the song of the nightingale, and if she didn't dazzle your eyes, she would charm your ears. I don't know what kind of offense led her to leave the Opéra-Comique and come to Variétés to act in a show created for her (meaning everything else was tossed aside to write this show). I still don't know why he entertained her delusion of playing the role of Roxelane in *The Three Sultans*. But they played music over the difficult-to-sing words, and with a lot of effort, a nothing of a show was made out of a mediocre show.

All of Paris rushed to see the deserter from Opéra-Comique. The place was a madhouse. It was cleaned from top to bottom, the box seats dusted off, and all charged to the Armenian. Nothing was spared.

Through the intervention of my friends, I got the show that the Théâtre-Français didn't want to put on at boulevard Montmartre to M. C.... With everything being done for the new prima donna, he didn't even thank me.

Mme. Ugalde made up for his rudeness. Her mind is quick, her personality charming, and I believe she has an excellent heart. The first time that I saw her up close, I was a bit disappointed, and the compliment that I had planned to give her on entering her room died on my lips.

Mme. Ugalde, you know, is rather short and very round. She has a limp, her eyes are dull, her mouth is wide, her lips protrude. The black dress she wore that night, with her hair up, made me think she was ugly at first sight. She very graciously asked me to sit down, giving me time to examine her at my leisure, to revise or change my opinion of her.

Women are coy with each other, and it's easy to see why. These are the most difficult conquests to win over.

Being a bad actress, I always played to raise the curtain. I was about to finish *The Queens of the Balls* when Boullé came to tell me, "Before you leave, go to Mme. Ugalde's. I'll take you to where she's staying."

Boullé was our stage manager. He was as tall and thin as the Armenian was short and fat. Boullé is stuttering, nervous, and sometimes irate, and the harder he tries, the more his tongue refuses to obey. We laugh, and he gets mad. However, he's a wonderful man and will forgive you very quickly for whatever stupid little things you say to him.

His intelligence and character are well known. Artists love him, and if he's a little plain, if he's reasonable with everyone, it's because, living in the middle of a difficult-to-govern republic, he wants to be on good terms with everyone.

His son, who acts under the name Nanteuil, is no more careful than anyone else. By chance we acted together in every production. I don't dare say that he was as bad an actor as I was an actress, but I do think it. But he was the most conscientious man, the best colleague I've ever known. Sometimes he had to dance with me, even though it wasn't so much his thing, but he set himself to it with such goodwill that he eventually was able to hop to the beat.

So I entered and went downstairs, because I was getting dressed on the second floor and the siren lived on the first. Boullé announced me and, as I said, Mme. Ugalde stood before me with a smile on her lips, no doubt to display her white teeth.

If she made a first impression of me, she surely found me stupid.

Not being in the habit of preparing what I was going to say, and having wanted to make an exception so I could politely engage the great singer with a compliment, I now found myself speechless as a child who has forgotten her manners. The idea didn't occur to me to say anything else. I wanted to take back my words at the sight of her. She went on getting ready as if I wasn't there.

Little by little, I came back to myself on seeing the white foundation, the red and black artistically composed, to create the lovely pink fairy of the Opéra-Comique. That gave me back my power of speech, and she tossed off a short trill in the middle of a phrase to warm up her voice. It returned to me my admiration for her.

But it was maybe too late. I didn't have any enchanting notes to throw at her feet like a shower of pearls. She asked me, laughing, if I thought she looked a little better. My embarrassment brought all my shyness back, and I once again wore the sour expression that betrayed all my most secret thoughts.

Mme. Ugalde, as usual, was very modest. She takes in everyone's opinion, and she has neither shame nor pride, which people think astonishing. She never begs to sing; she never subjects herself to the thousand usual precautions singers take to protect their voices.

On this day, she was ready. *The Three Sultans* was about to begin, and the room was full to bursting. She asked me to come hear her so I could tell her how she performed. At first I thought she was putting me on, but she insisted, and I went.

Her entrance was welcomed by a thunder of applause that went on for twenty minutes. Every time she opened her mouth to begin, the audience would clap as one. She was moved to tears and sang as only she sings, but it still surprised everyone the way she recited the verse. Not only was she a great singer, she was also a great actress, acting and singing with the grace of Augustine Brohan.

The cascade, the little flourishes, went on and on. The show was twice as long as it should have been.

The guest of honor was a tall and beautiful person, Mlle. Irene. That evening, she was stunning in her sultan's costume and her hair braided with golden sequins. Well, what do you think happened? Mme. Ugalde's talent had such great power over the masses, and her willpower was so strong that she could bend or break as she pleased. That evening, she was found to be more beautiful than this true beauty Mlle. Irene.

Kopp, who was playing the part of a eunuch, partnered with her so well that he contributed to her success. I saw him happy one time—just once—because he was in truth always glad to sacrifice himself a little.

The poor Baptiste from *The Bohemian Life* saw neither a higher salary nor more roles. This was unfair, and he would have been in the right to complain if it would have done him any good.

When I returned to Mme. Ugalde's dressing room, she was in costume for the final act, and I helped with an argument she was having with her hair stylist.

She had to enter dressed as a slave with her hair down. This, to put it mildly, was not easily done, as her hair was at least four feet long. It was almost like a cape around her. But she was set on the idea of having a hollow at the back of her head, and she absolutely insisted on filling the dimple on her neck that almost everyone had noticed.

Charles, the hairdresser, was desperate. He couldn't find anything to create the fake cavity. All of a sudden Mme. Ugalde yelled and laughed like a madwoman, and fell into one of the old office chairs.

"Here's my solution." She presented a fistful of old crinoline to the hairdresser, who recoiled in horror. Everyone was screaming again. She stomped her foot, but the coiffure artist held firm. He refused to include even a scrap of this rat's nest in the magnificent mane of the singer.

He was outnumbered. She asked each person if what she called her "pet" was so awful. When she asked Nargeot, the conductor of the orchestra (and composer of *Drin, Drin, Drin*), he said, "I've never seen anything like it." Nargeot is a bit deaf. He thought she was asking about her success.

In this show, which didn't do well despite the talent of the artist, there was a song that she sang marvelously. It began:

My sweet country, very dear France…

To hear her sing, I would have traveled to Belgium on foot. When I had finished my performance, I would wait in the wings to hear her, and Mme. Ugalde would tell me as she passed: "I'm going to sing for you."

One night when I was at my post—it was the twentieth show, I think—I was brought a little piece of paper folded like a ticket. I stood under an oil lamp and read with much effort:

Madame, it is absolutely necessary that I speak to you tonight. I'll only be free at ten thirty, at which time you'll find me in the galerie Vivienne, on the passage des Panoramas.

At first I thought this was a tactless lover. But

looking again, I recognized it as the writing of a woman—a woman who didn't really know how to write. Who could it be? Should I go or not? What do they want to see me about? I was definitely intrigued.

The simplest thing was not to go, but since women are often more curious than strategic, I left at exactly ten thirty, and I took care to look everywhere as I crossed the passage. I didn't see even the shadow of a woman, but I did see a young man who seemed to be coming toward me. I was about to get into a carriage on rue Vivienne when he said to me in the sweet voice of a child as he doffed his hat gracefully, "I'm the one who wrote to you. I would like to speak to you—I have to tell you something urgent, as you can see, because I didn't change out of my costume."

His hair was a beautiful black, styled yet curly, and overly pomaded in a way that I never liked in a man. He had a high forehead and a kind face, thin with a friendly smile. Altogether lovely.

When he mentioned his costume, I looked at him more carefully.

"You don't know me," he said with a smile, "or at least you don't recognize the little florist who worked on the rue du Temple, in the chorus at the theater Bellville."

51

AN OLD ACQUAINTANCE

THIS YOUNG MAN WAS A woman, and I didn't understand how I could have been fooled for a second.

I let go of my disagreeable attitude a little, but I couldn't get rid of it all at once. Many people have taken this for snobbishness, boastfulness, or pride that woman of my low station should not have.

My excuse, anyway, was justified by my error, and I took pains to apologize for my rudeness. I asked if she wanted to climb into my carriage so that we might be comfortable enough to chat. She accepted after telling me that she had come looking for me so that she could take me to the house of a women who wanted to see me before she died. I asked the name of this ailing woman, and she answered, "Rue d'Angoulême, at the corner of the boulevard."

And my coach headed off.

"Ah!" she said. "What mixed emotions I had on seeing you again! It cut off my ability to speak. I was almost afraid. What if you had been unkind? I never missed an occasion to see you at the Hippodrome or the theater. I've always followed you from afar and kept an ear open. Every one of your successes made me happy, and I wanted to tell you, but I had nothing and you were on the rise. You laugh, and maybe you're right to. The nuns who raised me told me I was a little nuts. I'm unique and I'm drawn to people, and I have a longer memory than most. That's all."

I was very flattered by her good memories of me, but I was even more intrigued to know whose house we were going to and who my companion was.

I asked her to tell me plainly who she was, because I didn't know the name of the sick woman, and she herself didn't bring to mind any memories of my own.

"I'm your age," she said. "I was born the same day as you. My given name is Elizabeth, like yours, and we did our apprenticeships at the same courtesan house on rue du Temple."

I remembered then and asked her what she was doing, and why she wore that costume.

Adèle's Story

God took my mother when I was young. I had nothing, and no help. The neighbors walked me around the quarter, inquiring at every door: "Does anyone have extra bread to give this child?"

My mother had died on rue Brody, and for a long time, every night the peddler on the boulevard at the door of the Ambigu-Comique gave me rye bread or cherries that she hadn't been able to sell that day.

Mme. Roger de B… heard about me. My misfortune touched her, and she placed me with the nuns. They had their work cut out for them with me. I missed my wandering ways, my independence. I was almost a vagabond. My care was too much like captivity. They got me an apprenticeship, and I learned the florist's trade.

Eventually, I fell in love with an artist. I thought he had more heart than talent, but I was wrong. Or, rather, I was suffering from my own delusion that I wasn't worthy of him. As long as he was happy, I was happy. If, at the time I knew him, he'd wanted to take my life, I honestly feel that he would have done something for me.

Anyway, I dreamed of the life of an actress. It became an impulse, an agitation, that didn't allow my heart to sleep, my mind to dream.

I was in the chorus at Belleville when you came to play the part of a poor girl in *Canal Saint-Martin*. But I was so unhappy at the time that I was planning to drown myself in the canal.

No one had any idea how depressed I was. I could go five days without eating. I was nice, I could sell myself like others did, but I would have rathered thrown myself in the canal.

It was a tough lesson for me, but she didn't know the details of my life. I asked why she never spoke to me at Belleville.

I was too depressed. I would have embarrassed you, or you would have given me charity, which would have embarrassed me. Besides, I wanted to die. I would have had the courage to go through with it if my strength hadn't left me. I sank like a stone.

When I came to, I was in a white bed at the Pitié hospital. They'd carried me there on a stretcher, and I realized I was so happy to stretch out under a blanket that I kissed my sheets. Then, when I saw a nun, my heart dropped. I remembered the nuns who had raised me, and I began to cry.

If I could have entered a convent then, I would have served the benevolent God on my knees all my life. But it required what I didn't have: sponsors or money.

When I was released from the hospital, Célestine came to find me in the theater. When she showed me the playbill, I saw your name on the list of ticket holders. I was let go from Belleville.

I found a little work, and I was about to leave the theater altogether, when the angel or devil on my shoulder had me run into someone who asked me to sing at cafés. They offered forty sous a day, and they would provide the costumes. I thought that was a good deal, so I accepted.

I had a contralto voice, but because I had to sing in any and every key, my voice broke. I left behind romantic roles to sing little songs dressed as a man. I'm always in a café. They say I bring in business, but I'm sure that money does not all go to me. Besides, I don't have any schooling, no one who taught me to count. That's why I'm often not able to help others as much as I want. If that weren't the case, I wouldn't have looked for you.

But I've been talking about myself for an hour when I should be talking about another more interesting person.

For several months, I have been staying in a hotel on rue d'Angoulême. After about two months there, a young woman came to live in the room next door. We were only separated by an old door. I heard everything the concierge said about a pregnant woman who couldn't go out and who lived on who knew what or how. I tried to see her, more out of curiosity than real interest. She seemed to stay hidden.

One morning I heard cries, and I went to her place. Someone ran to get the doctor. The poor woman was in labor until two in the morning. As it came into the world, her child seemed to eviscerate her insides.

As soon as she heard them say, "It's a girl," she fell into a coma.

The amazing thing is that the mother was pale and so thin you could count her ribs, but the baby was fat and pink and white. I gave the little girl to a wet nurse in the neighborhood. She was expensive, but I had no choice.

I had looked in my neighbor's drawers for something to dress the baby in and only found a mountain of pity. The drawers were empty, and I had paid for the first month of the wet nurse. I had done all I could, but nothing grandiose. The poor woman went from bad to worse. She made great efforts to write two letters, but neither received a response.

The last snub seemed to break her. I asked her a hundred times if she had parents or any friends who could come to her aid. She always said no. That night, I insisted more than ever.

"I had a friend once," she told me as she searched her memory, "but if my beloved friend abandoned me during a crisis, why would I try to find her now? Besides, even if she remembered me, it would be a sad memory. Go on, let me die! I don't have any right to anyone's mercy."

I mentioned her baby. She became a little more animated and said, "You're right. I want her placed at the home for foundlings. Céleste will know why. Go see her. You'll find her at the Variétés theater. She hasn't changed her name, and if her heart remains unchanged too, she will come."

We had arrived at rue d'Angoulême. Adèle—for that was the name of the flower girl—said as we got out of the carriage: "You should send your carriage back. You'll probably be here a while, and I'll find another for you when you want to leave."

I sent my coach away and followed her. The house was not elegant, the stairs were steep and narrow, and on each landing there were eight or ten numbered doors. These doors said a lot about the apartments, which were the size of tiny tobacco shops.

My heart was hammering. I followed Adèle in silence, but a world of ideas crossed my mind. When we reached the third floor, I had a thousand conjectures, each as far from the truth as the others.

Adèle carefully opened a door. I saw a small room, poorly furnished. Everything was in disarray. I couldn't see the sick woman clearly. A candle that she likely hadn't had the strength to extinguish burned on a painted wooden nightstand placed next to the headboard. It threw such a strange light on this woman and her things that I recoiled a step.

"Thank you for coming," she said in a voice that made me shiver. "Thank you. Tomorrow would have been too late."

I was already by the bed. I held the head of poor Denise in my arms. It was good for her that I found her in this state, this misery, my friend from prison. She was the first woman, maybe the only woman, who would have had a real attachment to me. She had led me into a bad life without knowing what she was doing, and she had since regretted it many times. At that moment, I saw her being so cruelly punished that the idea didn't occur to me for an instant to think she was the devil on my shoulder.

I cried, I laughed, and I was convinced that my presence brought her health and life.

Adèle placed a cup of tea on the nightstand, brought us a candle, gave me a seat, and went out. She said to me as she left, "If you need me, knock on the door, but don't talk too loudly if you have secrets, because I can hear everything that's said in here at my place."

Denise held my hands for a long time. I felt them warm up little by little. I waited until she was able to speak, because I couldn't find a word to say. I felt mute, devastated; I was truly face to face with death. The poor woman only sighed loudly and was so feeble that I thought she'd expired twenty times.

I went down to the concierge who was, I think, also the building manager, and I asked him to warm up a little sugared Bordeaux. I would have Denise drink a few sips of this wine. It would warm her up and bring back her strength and her memories.

Her eyes shone a little in their sockets, which were creased with suffering and depredation. Her jaw was outlined under her waxy skin, and I could count her teeth through her flesh, the only ornament left to her.

How things can change! An hour earlier, I wouldn't have believed it. Was this the poor girl, so fresh, so joyful, who had made me laugh when I wanted to cry? Who I had believed was happily married, and who I thought of so little in my affluence because I assumed she was beyond need? What had happened? I wanted to know, but I didn't dare interrogate her.

"Okay," she said, sitting up a little. "I have so many things to tell you that I don't know where to begin. If I faint, don't be afraid, just call Adèle. If you only knew how good she's been to me! It's the kind of heart you rarely meet in life. Without her, I'd be dead. A little earlier or a little later makes no difference to me, but the baby has a will to live, and I don't have a drop of milk. Adèle sold off or rented out her dresses to help me, and I think she keeps her men's costume because she doesn't have anything else to wear."

After a pause, Denise continued, "I don't have the courage or the strength to tell you the details of my life. I had a loving heart that led me toward all sorts of weaknesses. I was confident, and that became my downfall. I had my happiness in my hands, and I broke it like a child breaks a toy. I thought too much of myself and doubted others. Now I have nothing but the shadow of a hope, and I will not tell you things as I saw them, but how they stand today, when I know how it ends.

"Because I was shut into this room with my moral and physical desolation, my intelligence became sharp. I was sure that my judgment was fair and that I could teach women. Instead of telling them what I'm telling you, I would save them from shame by using myself as an example and a solution. But I'm going to carry to my grave my regrets and my wish to atone."

"In the end, you'll die forgiven, oui?"

Denise became so pale that I thought it was over. I began to ask God's forgiveness.

"I've sinned too much," she murmured. "A priest couldn't do anything for me. My destiny will follow me to the next world, as it already has in this one."

I didn't agree at all with this pathetic reasoning, but the late hour didn't leave me any time to send for a confessor. There should be, in these prayers said for your soul at the final moment, an infinite comfort for the forgiven. When everyone pushes her away, religion holds her hand, causes repentance to enter her heart, gives her faith, restores lost hope. If only at the last moment, it will help hold you up and teach you it's never too late to do good.

Denise was too smart not to understand this. I would have made her listen to reason if she could have heard me, but she began speaking again, and I didn't dare interrupt her.

DENISE'S STORY

I was thought to be ambitious and proud, but it didn't take me long to see my mistake. Deep down, I was made to be a housewife, not a courtesan. I latched onto things and made an interior life for myself out of nothing. I had some liaisons that started out fun and always ended with me in tears.

After eight years, I met a young man in Rouen. He was employed in a trading house. His mother was a little well-off, but this wouldn't amount to any great inheritance. I didn't consider him so far above me that we'd break up, since that always happened—when you come into wealth and a position in society, a status, you have to get married. His mother lived outside town. I lived with him and bore his name so that everyone knew we were together. He didn't earn much, but I took on most of the running of our little household, where we were happy. With my foolish confidence, I didn't see anything changing in our future. His name was Edouard M.... It wasn't a name that meant anything to anyone. Only my background as a courtesan kept me from marrying him, but I was convinced that I would eventually forget my past while making him forget it by dint of my kindness and sacrifice. For eight years, I was his servant, his slave, his genie in a bottle, the soul of his soul, the spirit of his spirit. He was promoted, hardworking, instructive to others, because I encouraged his work. I would never have left him. He wanted to marry me as soon as his mother was convinced that I loved him enough to be devoted to him and make him happy. He proposed to me many times, despite her objections, and I refused because I wanted to earn my happiness.

A year later, Edouard changed all of a sudden. He became dreamy, preoccupied, contradictory when he was with me. He was absorbed by work, he told me. His boss had left the business and made him head of the company. His mother very much wanted to see him in this job, but there was an obstacle in the way of all this: me.

An attempt was made to get me to understand, but my confidence—really my asinine stubbornness—didn't see it so clearly. I only understood that his status with me was not legal in the eyes of the world, so he wanted to marry me.

One day, I thought I would die from joy when I learned I was to be a mother. A baby would give me a new life, make everything else go away. This was forgiveness sent from God! Instead of smiling on hearing this news, Edouard became pale as death, and instead of taking my hand, he recoiled.

I had an inkling of my misfortune, but I didn't want to believe it. He had to spell it out for me through tears—

hypocritical tears, more cruel than a tossed-off insult.

"My mother learned everything about your past, my poor Louise (I had retaken my baptismal name), and she knew…A marriage between us is all but impossible, but I will not abandon you."

The idea of breaking up hit me so hard that I felt like I'd never get up again.

If he'd only blamed society, I would have understood, and maybe the sight of his child would change his mind. But he acted out of self-interest and ambition, and because he didn't love me anymore.

He had to shatter me to get rid of me and not wait, out of fear that my child was there. He picked a thousand fights with me, and I withstood it all for my baby. But one day, he brutally humiliated me. That day, he was worse than any other man! He berated me for a past that I had given up. This past, he said, didn't give him any assurance, any security. My child, my only strength, could be someone else's.

I had to repress everything to not kill this man, and stay strong to not go mad.

My fall will never be forgiven! Love, devotion, motherhood—nothing will raise me up again. He could commit the worst sins against me, be my pimp, insult me, get rid of me on a whim—none of this would change a thing about the esteem people have for him.

I thought things at the bottom were badly organized, and for the first time in my life, I had the guts to ask myself what I had done. It's true. But I had no idea how deep a pit I was throwing myself into.

I fled his house with only what I had on my back. I went to a hotel, hoping that he'd come looking for me. He sent along my things and fifty francs for travel expenses.

His mother came to see him and made him leave town. He didn't know when he'd be able to see me again and requested that I return to Paris, where he would send money as soon as he could. I waited a week in that hotel, a week that felt like a century.

I went back to check on his house, but he never returned. I went by several times at night, passing under the windows of our little rooms. My potted flowers still grew in the windows, but no one picked them. They fell and withered on the sill. My bird had been left to die in its cage. The bird, the flowers, the woman and child—all were going to end the same way.

I saw that there was no hope to hold on to anymore. I learned that he was going to marry the daughter of a businessman in Elbeuf and that he was counting on her dowry to fund his business. So I came back to Paris and decided to work to feed my child. Without bitterness, I took stock of how I'd been sapped of strength and found a little work, but I fell ill. I'm twenty-eight years old. A first pregnancy at this age is hard on your body. I regretted going so far from him; I should have stayed nearby, like the very embodiment of blame. But I didn't have the strength to go back yet again. My savings were being used up little by little, so I stayed here to save money. I wrote letter after letter to Rouen, not to ask for anything for myself but for my baby, who would suffer from our poverty. No one answered.

Not a bit of help, not a word of consolation, came to me from him. He was happily married. He didn't have time to remember me, and I'm telling you, without this kind girl, it would all be over. Without her, I would not have thought of you. I no longer have the strength for any of it.

She let her head droop as if it were inert. I was afraid, but she opened her eyes again and gestured for me to give her something to drink. Then she took up her tale again.

"In any case, destiny or accident came back to bite us. I'm going to tell you what I can't tell others because they wouldn't understand."

I asked her to rest and assured her that I would do all I could for her and her child.

"Me," she said with a smile. "The only thing I need anymore is a scrap of fabric and some pine boards. I don't want you nor any other woman to take on my child. I know that you would never treat her badly, but no one is capable of always doing what they wish. I would find the strength to smother her if I knew for certain that she would become what I've been. I found her a home where foundlings can find a family, regular care, and a good role model. The idea of evil will never occur to them."

This word *foundlings* scared me for a week. Then I got used to it as I went back over my memories.

I had never met, among the courtesans, a young girl who'd been raised at Orphelines. Then I remembered having seen them sometimes, all dressed the same and walking in a row down the street. They were led by the nuns, who tended nonstop to this troop that had been abandoned by mankind. All these children seemed happy. The serenity of their souls was transparent on their faces. Not one little girl looked around her. They believed themselves to be children of God, I'm sure of it, and that's better than knowing her mother and being ashamed of her.

I fought against this solution. The foundlings institution—which I had never considered, it's true, from this point of view—seemed sadder and more depressing to me than all the courtesan houses, but I could hardly oppose the last wish of a dying mother who saw only a route to respect for her daughter.

I resolved, however, to hold out for her being near her father. Taking advantage of a moment when Denise was resting, I wrote a long letter to one of my friends who lived in Rouen. I outlined for him as well as I could the sad situation of this poor abandoned girl.

The subject and setting were designed to inspire me to write touchingly! I added a few lines for M. Edouard to the letter—reprimands, requests, and threats. I was sure of having some kind of response from my friend, but would he arrive in time?

52

DENISE

I SENT FOR A DOCTOR at the break of day. He said that the patient could not be transported to my house, that her state had deteriorated too far. However, she could live several more days if she was given the medicines he prescribed.

I got to know the little girl. She was sweet and stubborn. Adèle had bought her a pretty little layette and went to see the baby twice a day to be sure she lacked nothing. Adèle has one of those personalities that can't be described. You have to see for yourself how simple, how self-contained she is to believe it.

I wanted to make sure she knew that I saw what she'd done for Denise. She answered that if Denise died, she would keep the baby. She wasn't rich, but she would do her best and work a little more. She would do as she said, and I was quite sure that she would carry through with all her heart on what she started.

I went back to see Denise that same day. She was much worse.

That night, they thought it was all over. I was sent for at midnight. Adèle was dabbing at Denise's temples with vinegar.

"She had a terrible setback," she said quietly. "It's tonight."

Denise signaled that she saw me, but she couldn't speak to me. I stayed near her bed without daring to say a word. She slept for a few hours, but was restless in her sleep. She tossed and turned and murmured unintelligibly.

Soon gargling, raspy sounds came from her throat, then weak, strangled cries and whimpering like a baby. At five o'clock, she sat up, her cheeks hollow and pale, and seemed a little more awake.

"I'm coming back to life." She smiled. "I dreamed it."

She spoke again, but her words expired between her teeth and her chest heaved. I had seen the mother of my goddaughter die, and I understood that the final moment was approaching. I asked her if she wanted to receive the sacraments, and she shook her head no.

"Her daughter is not yet baptized," Adèle said to me quietly.

I asked the building's maid to go to Sainte-Élisabeth to look for a priest and to quickly fetch the baby's wet nurse.

So as not to scare Denise, I told her that I was going to rock her baby while we waited for the regular baptism ceremony.

At seven o'clock, the priest arrived. We left him alone with the ailing woman. He spoke with her for a long time in a low voice, urging her, surely, to pray and be brave. Denise found her tears and her words. She must have wanted to kneel to ask God's forgiveness, because we heard the priest say to her, "You aren't strong enough to kneel. Later, my child, you will pray to the Lord as he commands you to pray. In the meantime, I will pray for you."

When we came back in, she was calm. Her face held an expression of serenity that she hadn't had an hour before. When a nervous tremor betrayed her pain, she kissed a small crucifix the priest had placed near her to bring her strength.

The infant received her first unction in the room where her mother received her final unction. Denise watched it all without saying a word. A fat tear rolled down her cheek, and I believe she was praying in her mind. The priest promised to come back to see her.

I had asked my maid to bring me any communication from Rouen, and at nine o'clock, she brought me a letter. It was my friend. Here is a little of what it said:

My Dear Céleste,
I put myself at your disposal, and you were right to reach out to me. I'm sorry that the mission you sent me on was so easy to fulfill. If I get credit for anything, it's promptness.

I went around to Edouard M…'s suite. It was his mother who let me in; she made me wait almost an hour. She was sent to me with an excuse. Her son, she told me, was dangerously ill. There were at the moment two doctors at his bedside, and she was anxious to learn the results of their consultation. Her son had done something reckless during his work at the factory, the result being a returning fever that might drive him to the tomb.

The poor woman gushed a fountain of tears, and I had to wait until she was little more settled to explain the reason for my visit. The timing, however, was lucky, and I couldn't find any better way to do it than to give her your letter. Her tears doubled, which didn't surprise me. I had cried myself as I read it.

I added to my reading of the letter some personal touches: "M. M... is behaving badly," I told her. "What he has done are the actions of a heartless man. This poor thing had no parents, no support. Well, from this day on, she has a friend, a protector, in me, and if your son doesn't do what an honest man should in these circumstances—give bread to a child who only wishes to live, a child that he created in his pleasure knowing he would abandon her— then I would tell him to his face what I think, and I will take what comes for it."

"Ah!" cried this good woman, who hadn't seemed like a snob at heart. "You would dare to provoke my son for a loose woman he found who knows where?"

"If you don't know, he should. He went there. And this 'loose woman' shared his name for seven years. She is the mother of his child, and he should respect her if he respects himself. If he doesn't want to marry her, he's free to make that choice. However, his conscience seems to me to be very flexible. He must do something for this poor woman as he deserts her. She gave him seven years of her love, of her youth. You can't do something like this over and over in your life. It must be paid for.

"You'll be told it's too late to save her, there's nothing that can be done for her. But her child remains. Would you let her go to a shelter like a dog? If you do that, God will punish you. And who knows if it won't begin to affect your son."

"Monsieur, don't say such things!" cried this respectable woman with her hands clasped. "You'll make me go mad. My poor Edouard is not heartless. He hasn't even seen the latest letters from Louise. I received them and recognized the handwriting. I burned them without reading them. If I had known that she was so badly off, I myself would have been in Paris. Poor little girl! If I am about to lose my son, that's all I would have left of him.

"Where does Louise live? Paris? I want to write to her, to beg her to give me the child—my child. I will take good care of her. I will love her with all my heart to right the wrongs I've done her mother.

"You're right, God is punishing me, and maybe about to do me the same wrongs I've done to another. As she herself cannot come, listen: My Edouard is married, but let her entrust her daughter to you. Ah, if only I could go to Paris! But I must stay here.

"I'm too old to suffer any more. The least shock will shatter me. If my son should die tomorrow, I would wish I'd died today."

"You no longer have that right," I said. "You have another child."

And with that, I returned to my house to write to you. What do you want to do?

Can I be of use in some way? I am entirely at your disposal.

I read this letter to Denise several times. She gripped my hand with the little strength she had and said, "He suffers…It does me good to know that he never received my letters. May God forgive him as I forgive him the wrongs that he's done to me! My daughter must be taken there soon. I want him to see her at least once."

I went to fetch the wet nurse. Denise gave her daughter one long, last kiss. Her lips stayed open, her eyes stayed open. She had died. Not in despair, as she would have if chance hadn't brought me to her bedside, but in faith, a smile on her lips and her heart full of hope.

The wet nurse left at noon or one. When she saw the child being carried off, Adèle wept. She already thought of it as hers. It is so natural to have all-consuming affections when you're a woman who's been tossed onto the earth without family, like a ship launched onto the sea without sails, always seeking to create lasting compassion.

"Well," she said to me as she dried her tears, "happiness escapes me yet again. It seems that if I was put here to complete some task, I would have done something good by now."

The priest who had assisted Denise returned later that day, as he had promised. He prayed for a while over the deceased and sat vigil for several hours, saying the prayer of the dead. I had no doubt that he had earned grace before the one who will judge us all.

As for me, it seemed that the exhortations of this sainted man made me better, too.

Two days later, I received a letter from Rouen that assured me that everything had been done on behalf of my poor friend's baby. The infant's arrival was celebrated by Edouard's mother. She immediately saw a resemblance to her son.

But the joy didn't last long. The fever and delirium of his illness took hold. He didn't recognize either his mother or his wife, and he died in their arms twenty-four hours after Denise died.

The good woman began to shower all her affections on the infant. She would be rich one day. Here was an innocent who didn't bear any of the sins of the mother: This is fair, and so rare.

The death of Denise hit me hard, but in the midst of my anguish and preoccupations, I had little room for feeling sorry. Besides, when you've seen birth and death all around you, you get used to death. And what seems like a huge event at the beginning of life seems less remarkable in the natural course of things, I think, by the time you reach the end. There are beings for whom death is a deliverance. I considered Denise luckier than me; instead of feeling sorry for myself at her passing, I envied her.

The miserable life where I had found her still fueled my fear of the future.

※

The day of the revue's premiere arrived. I had to sing a great rondo. I'd worked hard—the role was serious, I understood it well, and for the first time since I'd become an actress, I felt at ease.

The public rewarded my efforts. I was showered in applause and called back for two encores. The bravos were music to my ears.

But alas! Glory is fleeting, and there are two sides to every coin. At the third performance, I sang a half step flatter than the orchestra. I was off the whole time, but that was only an accident. I had shocked everyone the day of the premiere. My place was assured; I had waited long enough.

It was a little after this that I received the first of the letters that Robert had written from the sea. At the time, they were both very good and very bad for me. I was glad to see that the memory of me grew in his thoughts the farther he traveled from me, but this sweet pleading from so far away tugged at my heart.

For several months I put my wide-ranging and poignant emotions to the test. My physical strength, despite my natural energy, couldn't withstand it. He brought on a terrible reaction. I fell ill, so ill that I had to take a break from the theater. I left after the eighteenth show.

M. D... came to see me. He knew that I didn't want my role anymore. He was hoping to make me change my mind.

He had become one of my best friends, and he was very good to me during this illness. The affection that I extended to him proved that he wasn't like the others to me. I was always afraid of spending time with writers and actresses.

In the theater, there are a lot of conscientious writers who only see the grand facets of the art. There are sadly some who use their intelligence to satisfy their worst impulses. Young people falsely think of themselves as great men because they hold a pen, and they envy to the point of hatred anyone whose talent they can't match! It's a mix of misplaced emotion, unfairness, and rebellion.

A few have a particular way with words; they almost seem to speak a different language. So, to express their satisfaction with themselves, they say, "I have enough presence, eh? We are the sons of the family! The men of the world are but deer! We're the only ones in line."

They hound the actresses so badly they take everything from them, including their shadows. Their main means of seduction consists of saying to women from the theater that they alone are the *true great ladies*. They'll make you all kinds of miserable. Often you just let them in because you can't do anything else. They don't want women of modest renown. It's unworthy of them. They must be the most elegant women, the biggest names. It costs them so little, and they are so complacent. But if the actress, who is almost always also a courtesan, doesn't throw his golden cape under his feet with appropriate shame, if she doesn't leave everything behind to go with him to a seedy bar, to watch him smoke his pipe, he plots his revenge.

They grab her, waiting behind a curtain, deceiving the stage manager so that they might leave. They take over her apartment, drink wine that she paid for from her glass. When they drink, they insult even the décor. This goes on for a few months without it costing him even a kind word.

That's not all. You have to lose half your life to laughing and drinking.

They write a pamphlet, a bit of verse, a play about puritanism. To know women, you have to live with them, they say. That's a lie and a shitty excuse. Men of expansive minds judge them and damn them, having seen the product of their embarrassing lives. When the moralist is a boyfriend who hits me, he's sure that he'll get away with it. He doesn't even have the semblance of an argument as an excuse, and it disgusts me.

I knew all of these men, who are dependent on these women they now condemn. They're the most relentless.

I get my own justice.

I kiss the ground before a respectable woman. I don't respond to admonishments from a fair man, no matter how serious they are. I will explain my whole life to him. I promise him that I have done worse than anyone around, that I'm a terrifying creature, that me and those like me—we become the terrors of good men. But when one of those men who helps when a woman first falls from grace insults me in order to be invited to another's house, I look him in the face and laugh as I say, "I forgive you the insult because you have to make a living. How much were you given? I understand the market for notoriety. Look: Don't bullshit me and tell me that you want to fix a world while you're mining everything out of it."

These guys are rare exceptions, but they exist.

M. D... was an honest man full of scorn for the literati, and he never wanted to make the theater a vehicle for petty revenge.

53

PREMONITIONS

My illness brought up all my sadness, all my disappointments, all my bitterness.

One day followed the last, and I didn't receive any news from Robert.

I had begun to imagine dire situations when I received a bunch of letters at once, all giving me sad details and making me feel even less reassured.

18 August 1852

I don't know, my dear Céleste, if we'll ever see each other again!

Such is life. It's full of fleeting joys and lasting depressions, of relationships begun and broken up.

By a strange coincidence, these relationships never happen at a time when they might last.

You discover the heart that you've been looking for the day that heart stops beating.

A thousand things, a thousand accidents, separate loving souls during a lifetime. Then comes the separation of death that undoes all our plans…

Come on, heart, stop begging and don't hammer out the melancholy of memory along with false hopes.

If your sorrows are as large as your love, then your courage will be as high as your depression is low.

You're at the opposite end of the earth, and your cries will never reach me and rend the heart that has made you suffer so much.

And even they reach me, will they reverberate like an echo?

Maybe cries of joy and celebration.

And so I endure them without excuses, and may your only words be words of forgiveness and tenderness.

This love is not beautiful or more pure in this land, far from the joys, the laughs, the orgies that could dirty it and humiliate it through contact—far from Paris, far from the world where devotion is stupid, tenderness is foolish, and faithfulness is ridiculous.

19 August 1852

I am suffering so much that discouragement has overtaken my soul.

The boat that should have left for England two weeks after us has not arrived.

I cannot set off for the mines in the state I'm in; besides, I would like to be here when this ship comes in as I hope to receive news from France.

I wrote to my family regarding the situation where I

find myself, and I'm also waiting for M. L…, the young man I spoke of in my first letters.

My nights are awful, full of dreams—nightmares—where your face appears. You could say it sits at my headboard and takes pleasure in breaking my heart.

I get up and, however feebly, I take up the pen again to write to you.

I lack the words to compose my thoughts, yet my heart has so many things to tell you. I want so much to see you, to chat with you for a long while.

I know that my appeals weigh on you, and they will not reawaken an expired love in your heart, but I love to live on anguish.

I want to express all this violence to you.

Oh! If only I were loved! I would find, when I spoke to you, a language worthy of heaven.

Words escape me because your soul doesn't understand my soul.

I can't anymore.

The physical pain shatters my morals. I am so alone. I don't even dare ask for a doctor because I can't pay him.

And the ship that should deliver L…, and the letters, hasn't come!

It is so nice, when you're down, to have a friend. He extended a hand in friendship to me. His presence will be a great comfort.

May you be happy!

26 August 1852

No news! No ship!

I thought I was going to tell you in this letter that I'd left for the mines, but I cannot leave Sydney without having received any news from France.

Céleste, Céleste, I do not deserve a souvenir from you, and if my name sometimes intrudes on your joy and pleasure, at least try to treat it with some respect.

I'm going to wait another few days, until the end of the week. If the ship I'm waiting for hasn't arrived, I'll set out on the road to the mines.

Sydney, 20 September 1852

I'm getting on a horse in an hour.

I used up the last of my money. After having sold everything I have to buy a horse, I'm leaving for the mines.

I'm going into the earth two hundred miles from here.

It will take me eleven to fifteen days to get there.

I have a feeling I won't make it.

Beyond the fatigue from the journey, it's a job so hard that I don't think I can take it. Even if I do, the deck is stacked against my success.

I don't want to start down this road, Céleste, without sending my last farewells to you, the only love of my life and whose memory and thoughts will stay with me as long as I live.

You might say that my love for you is stronger due to the wrong you've done me.

I love you now as I have always loved you.

Pity me, for I suffer very much, and cling to the only good memory you have.

I should hate you. I adore you.

Goodbye, my idol! I'm sending this final remembrance to you as if I should never see you again. Why wish it?

What would you give me now?

When I had everything that could make you proud of my love, you looked down on it.

Now I'm ruined, my hair has turned white, my heart is broken, the future is nothing.

Farewell, farewell, I love you! Goodbye, I forgive you.

I'm tossing this letter in the mail on my way out of Sydney.

Goodbye, and don't forget that at the end of the earth, there is a heart that beats only for you. Adieu!

Robert

I often wrote to Robert, but my letters had nothing like the same fiery eloquence as his.

They were nothing like the letters I'd posted to Berry. The former were ardent, impassioned; the latter, cold and colorless.

Was this a sign of not caring anymore? Everyone believed him and maybe even blamed me. But the hearts of women are mysteries, and everyone was wrong. My soul was too troubled, too deeply upset to show it.

Robert stared down his depression and the magnificence of nature, his eyes fixed on the ocean, while writing me beautiful letters full of poetry and sweetness! And me, lost among my red tape, under the weight of a thousand hurtful gazes, I folded up on myself. I only had the strength for a silent depression.

Besides, I didn't know where Robert was.

I wondered if my letters could even reach him.

Surely it's a personality flaw, but this uncertainty froze my thoughts.

Time, which is the master of all, dissolved my illness better than the art of medicine.

As always, my physical convalescence had not caused any kind of moral convalescence.

I regained a little confidence and courage.

The wounds Robert had given me scarred over little by little.

If it weren't so depressing, this would have lasted longer, maybe for the rest of my life. But I was so depressed that when one of the bad thoughts from the two years I was involved in his ruin crossed my mind, I shooed it away. In spite of myself, I felt a tenderness for him return—a tenderness that my revenge had entirely snuffed.

Women who, like me, violated indecency laws are forced to blush at their thoughts as well as their actions.

The image of Robert was not the only one that came to mind.

I wrote many letters to Richard, which went unanswered.

I was quite sure, however, that he hadn't forgotten me. But it was his kind, sweet soul's nature to tend to his sadness in solitude. During his travels in California, he had gone two years without writing to me. I had no right to force the thought of me onto this suffering soul.

He lived in my heart, which was so unworthy of him. Poor Richard! If I had only given him all the love he deserved, if he should from here on remain a stranger in my life, I would still keep a significant place for him in my thoughts. He never caused me harm.

I often mourned the love that I had for Robert, love that we'd both lost because, thanks to his making me miserable with his whims, he had killed—suffocated—my passion, my confidence. My heart was shredded and then hardened through humiliation. I thought I was always under attack, so I was always fighting back.

I loved Richard like a brother. I would have helped him even if it cost me my blood. Now his memory perfumed my life, just as the night that had passed at his rival Robert's was hell to him.

He continued to cause a major transformation in me, but nothing was more changeable than my mood. Sometimes he made me want to retreat to a corner to live alone, like a wild animal.

Poor fool! Didn't I already have a chain to drag around?

I had to play at happiness when I felt like dying from wanting to cry. I had to sell smiles, and I was all out.

I had to say to every woman who asked, "Oh, hey! How is your case going?": "It's going marvelously. I'm sure I'll win it all."

Meanwhile, at the bottom of my soul, I was being eaten alive by worry. I had to deal with inconvenient friends who could have protected me or advised me, had to listen to the most ridiculous pronouncements.

When a woman is merely passable to society, she's imposed on and given nothing. She's left to fall one step lower. So then you have to create a ruse and become an expert diplomat to resist all these pretensions for yourself without running into those who have them. The most hostile of my enemies was a rejected lover.

Sometimes I went so far as to put together a plan to leave the country. Not being able to escape myself, I at least wanted to be able to escape the country where I had wasted my life.

I found the traces of these thoughts in one of my letters to Robert.

I also found the traces of my angry movements that memories of the past caused me to make against him.

> *It's nine o'clock in the evening.*
>
> *I'm by the fire in the dressing room where that woman waited the day I was crying on this bed so hard that now it feels like a tomb.*
>
> *Since that day, I see you following my every step. You left the apartment to me, but since then, I've never been happy. The memory of a few hours has killed my entire life with you.*
>
> *And when I think of your weakness for that woman, the way you left me, my heart races and my head burns.*
>
> *I laugh, and I'm happy for your* misery.
>
> *I've suffered so much. And this scar that you both laughed at is often still painful!*
>
> *I don't have a hate-filled heart, but I detest that creature from whom I asked grace and to whom the eruption of our fight gave a halo.*
>
> *I probably won't live long enough to see their misery, these snarky women, but if I outlast all my afflictions, I'll get my revenge in the future.*
>
> *As soon as my court cases are finished, I am going on a long voyage. I will leave this country. I will be a foreigner.*
>
> *I don't want to set up any theater jobs here, nor in London. London is too close.*
>
> *When it's all finished, I'm gone.*
>
> *To go anywhere near you is impossible. It would only link our depressions.*
>
> *You won't do anything in this country during your years of exile.*
>
> *I won't be around when you return. Whether I'm dead or just gone, my soul will be near you to say, "Be*

brave. You should have hope. You're still young; you have millionaires as brothers and sisters. They can't abandon you completely. They'll want to make you submit to them and atone, but don't think of it as harsh. They have noble hearts; they will open their arms to you. There is still a star on the horizon—never take your eyes off it. Your environment was once full of piety. Return your thoughts to God once again."

As for me, everything is darkness. I have the feeling you don't love me anymore, that your depression removed from your heart a love that was not made for me. Maybe another has replaced me. If she makes you happy, so much the better.

My letters were not always friendly.

There was goodness and kindness, I told him:

If all these depressing trials were over, I would leave this disgusting scene, which I scoff at, because it is the worst of all worlds.

It flatters silly people, it's vice without need, without passion, without excuse.

Rudeness and depravity rule over what they call parties and fun.

You have to blush for yourself when necessity brings you in their midst.

If you find me still deserving, I will be able to join you on the other side of the earth.

You'll be older, you say. That's fine, and maybe better. I wouldn't love you any less.

You'll be everything to me. We'll be locked away in the same corner of the world.

No one will remember when we were young; we'll

forget it ourselves.

I've fallen very ill, and I'm afraid of dying, solely because of you. I'm afraid of not seeing you again.

My life for you! Maybe it be long enough to ransom the past.

While I waited, the theatrical path I followed was so dry that I often wanted to quit.

Without Page, I think I would have left the theater altogether. Sadly, she became ill and left Variétés. My only friend gone. Boredom overcame me more than ever.

I looked for distractions from my boredom. I was forced to answer the disparaging attacks made by my opponents, to make notes on my life, notes indispensable to my court case. I ended up taking a liking to this scribbling.

I defended myself better in writing than by speaking. In the face of the injustices of which I was a victim, I exhibited an effortless passion that won over anyone who was interested in me.

At that moment, however, I still believed that all was lost. Cleverness, so it was thought, was on the side of men. Nothing stopped them, and I often searched my thoughts to see if they didn't have a mysterious reason for this relentless, disloyal war.

Hate seemed to edge out reason in those who came after me.

I mentioned that in my absence, they'd come into my house, open my cupboards, go through my papers and my most private letters, and take whatever seemed like ammunition against me.

I brought new legal arguments with the prosecutor, but justice had so much to do that I thought for a second she was going to stop before she got to me.

I was at the point of giving it all up when the harmful attacks directed at Robert gave me new energy. It wasn't only my money; for him, it was about honor. He was accused of fraud. They said that, when he saw he was about to go broke, he had used me as a scapegoat.

The trial started up again. For three months the papers were only occupied with this business and publicly linked my name to his genteel name. But he couldn't be brought any lower; he was already broke. Besides, Robert was in exile and so unhappy that he had already atoned for half his wrongs.

I couldn't listen to them insulting him. I tried to be eloquent in defending him.

I must say that if a friend or family member had secured about a thousand francs for him at this time, all this would have been taken care of without my getting involved, and my name would not have been linked to his at every turn to wither it on the vine.

Some letters I'd written to Robert and that were known to be at my house, along with papers that he left with me when he left the country, were part of the case. They were published in *Le Droit* and were contested. They were too well written, they said, to have come from my brain. They had in fact been dictated to me, yes?

I had to prove myself by talking out all my thoughts. Instead of weakening my resolve, this made me more sure, more thoughtful.

I began to understand that a lifetime of hard work helps you get through anything. Torture can even become interesting at a certain point.

I wasn't sleeping, I barely ate, but I had a goal: to prove that what I owned was mine, and that Robert could waste money, but he was incapable of plotting, of even having come up with the cynical calculations they were accusing me of. Finally, I had to defend a small fortune that would secure my future and give me the means to honorably raise the child God seemed to have sent me.

I've mentioned that, in both the happy and sad times in my life, I had the habit of writing down my thoughts.

A friend paid me to take stock of my entire past life, to make a confession that would enlighten my judges. So I wrote out my life in the hope of making my defense easier.

A few years earlier, I would not have understood what was being asked of me; a few years later, I wouldn't have had the time.

But at that moment, for this fermentation of my mind, I could take stock of all my challenges without flinching.

Study all day, write all night—nothing could stop me.

I set myself to this task, and I found an interest in it that surprised and enchanted me.

As I went back over my life, I was surprised to see the bitterness fade.

I discovered two strengths in myself that I had never doubted, and I understood that there could be, outside of a hectic life, joy and happiness.

I had a kind of premonition that the final phase of my life was being prepared.

Not only did the memories of my past come back, but this unexpected happiness seemed to draw in the people I still thought of with affection.

One day, my chambermaid said that there was a soldier in the salon who wanted to see me.

"I asked his name," she said, "but he answered, 'Your mistress surely has forgotten it.'"

My curiosity piqued, I went to see this mysterious visitor.

Imagine my surprise—it was Deligny! Deligny, who I'd been told was dead! Deligny looking well and wearing an officer's uniform! I circled around him three times without saying a word.

"Don't you recognize me?" he said. "Do I have to give you my card?"

"Oui, of course I recognize you, but I'm a little shocked to hear you speak. They told me you were dead."

"Me!" he said with a laugh. "I would have sent you notice if so, but thank God, I'm fine. I've been in Paris for two days. I couldn't put off seeing you any longer. May I kiss you?"

"Please do."

"I've changed," he said, placing a hand on my hip. "It's hot down where I've been, and I eat wild cattle. All the same, it's over, and I'm fine with it. I'm stationed at the military academy. I'm a little underdressed today," he added as he turned around. "There's a formal uniform that is beautiful. I'll put it on when I come to see you again, if I may."

"Certainly, my good Deligny, as often as you like. You seem so happy that I don't even need to ask if you are. Are you still picking fights?"

"Nothing's changed," he said as he took my hands, "and my affection for you has changed less than anything else."

I laughed incredulously.

"There's no great honor in not changing for love in that country," he said, "where the women have skin like black licorice, and if you stand too close when speaking to them, there's a good chance her Bedouin husband wants to put a bullet in your head for it. But that's no excuse. I would never love any other woman but you."

I laughed again, and he went on.

"I hear myself. There's love, and there's love. Sometimes they make fun of me in our quarters, but I tell them I'm not alone. No more is said, because everyone knows I will not hear jokes about you. And you, are you happy, Céleste?"

"Oui, my friend, happy to see you."

"Well," he said, kissing my hands, "even better! I didn't dare come because I know that you're an actress, that you have a whole entourage, that you have horses and carriages. Speaking of which, I'd like to see you on stage. Ah! You don't know. Poor Médème died. He was killed in a duel. Everyone thinks it was me."

"That's how I heard wrong, then. Poor boy, he was so sweet."

"Bah, we don't have to think of it. It could happen to anyone. It's better to go out like that than in the hands of a doctor. But it's getting late, and I'm dining in the city, so I must leave you. Au revoir, my lovely Céleste, we'll dine together one of these days. I'll introduce you to my friends, good children all. They know of you, I spoke of you down there. Adieu, see you soon!"

I watched him go. I can't tell you the pleasure I felt on seeing him so happy. I felt a real joy, which hadn't happened to me in a long time.

I also had hope that some kind of help would be sent to my poor Robert. My illusions on this matter would not last long.

Just as Deligny left, I was brought a stack of letters

from Australia. I ripped open the envelope with a premonition of sadness. I was sure that reading them would affect me.

54

THE AUSTRALIAN MINES

DIARY OF A MINER

I left Sydney at eight o'clock in the morning with a Frenchman, M. Malfil…, who like me was headed for the mines. The road up to Paramatta was charming.

I had no luck at all. My horse began to get sores on his rear and back.

Lunch was in Paramatta in an inn with local drinks.

We got back on the road and arrived on the outskirts of Perth after riding ten miles.

We crossed a river.

The landscape changed and became more severe.

The road rose, and there was a massive flock of ravens.

We entered a forest with gigantic trees like I've never seen in Europe.

In one sweep, the eye plunges into the gorges lost

from view. And as we climbed higher, we saw behind us the plains and prairies that we had crossed.

The entire time that my imagination took flight, my heart and thoughts returned to Céleste.

I picked a sprig of sweet-smelling heather by the side of the path, promising to send it to you in my next letter.

At six o'clock that evening, we were overtaken by both rain and nightfall.

The further we got from Sydney, the worse the road got. Finally, half on foot and half on horseback, we arrived at Blue at seven o'clock. My poor horse was injured all along his back.

However, thanks to a good fire for me and a stall for my horse, we can—I hope—set out again tomorrow.

At four thirty we met a cart with four horses coming from Bathurst. It had an escort.

It was a load of gold.

We also came across some miners who were coming back on horses, and we found an equally large number camped in the middle of the bush with immense fires around their horses and carts.

These encampments are very innovative, and all through the night, they have the most singular effect.

They say there are camps of thieves in the middle of these massive woods.

I witnessed a spectacle so strange, so new to me, that I'm going to try to describe it.

The Miner's Camp

In a lonely ravine, at the edge of a little creek, five miners met up.

The moon was shining bright in the sky, and as its

rays passed through the branches of the gigantic pines, they mixed with the red light of the fire around which these five associates were grouped.

They served supper.

The faces and accouterments of these individuals were most remarkable. Schiller never dreamed of these brigands, with their tanned faces, their scruffy hair and beards. Never did the pencil of the fantasist Callot depict such tattered rags, such filthy shoes.

Each individual was an arsenal unto himself: pistols, revolvers, knives, daggers. Their belts were lacking nothing. They were kitted out like guys in a low-class street theater. In the Australian forest, they were terrifying.

These men were, however, inoffensive diggers (that is, miners) having a little meal after a long day of travel. The conversation was loud, their gestures fast and jerky.

I thought for a second they would just as soon fight as talk.

One of these men was stretched out in the grass, his head resting against a tree trunk. He seemed to be in a bad way. His friends called him Meurice and offered him a drink.

Meurice was of a higher class than the others, but his illness had taken a considerable toll on him. He was paler than the moon, his cheeks were sunken, and his eyes were almost lifeless. He seemed to take no part in his friends' conversation.

"Paul," he said to one of them, "I'm thirsty."

Paul glanced at him with both interest and pity. He passed him a tin cup full of hot tea and brandy, which he swallowed in one gulp.

"You want grog, Cartahu?" Paul asked a fat boy who was looking at a small gold nugget folded inside his leather purse. The day had been fruitful. There was satisfaction in Cartahu's eyes.

Paul's face was cold, unlike those of his companions. His hair and beard were gray, and deep wrinkles creased his forehead. He was old before his time. You could tell he drank to forget.

A bottle of brandy was passed from hand to hand and mouth to mouth.

Our three other friends went to refill the bottle each time it was emptied at a barrel on a little platform about five feet high.

The drunkenness set in. Paul himself drank in huge gulps.

"Come," he said to each as they drank. "Let's not drink to forget, like everyone else, but to taste the poison that brings eternal rest. Come on, comrades, drink another: to lost friends, to our memories, to our sadness, to our hopes."

"Hold on," cried Cartahu, "I have an idea: to our last mistresses."

Two or three bottles of brandy were upended into a tin plate that was used to pan for gold. They set it on fire. They swallowed this horrible strong punch like it was pure water, until they were equally sloshed. Only Meurice and Paul didn't throw up.

Meurice settled into a corner. Paul seemed to be struck dumb, his eyes staring and a scornful smile on his lips.

"I want to hear the story of le Faucheux," Cartahu said, gesturing toward a man built like a stalk of asparagus. "You go first, then Mobile will tell us a story after."

"I'm thirsty," slurred Meurice.

"Order it," answered Cartahu.

"Pass the tea to the softie," added Mobile as he lifted his cup of grog. He choked on it with a fit of coughing.

"Gentlemen," exclaimed le Faucheux, "we've been prospecting together for a year, sleeping badly under the same tarp, and not comfortably. The gang's pile of loot grows higher, and the time of our bittersweet parting draws near. No one speaks of his past, of course. They have little secrets they don't want to divulge. As they cross the border, they carry a new passport, a new name, and a new life to the frontier.

"But the future, gentlemen, the future with your wealth, which we can feel with our fingers, how can each of us listen to the call of this new life? Come, children of our land, the day of confession has arrived. Each of us trots out his little rosary and asks again that author of the most original plan walk in triumph around this sacred fire!"

"Hurrah!" cried Mobile and Cartahu.

"I have the honor of providing an example," le Faucheux continued, "to explain to the honorable assembly my plan for the future. I ask, before I begin, and to clarify my thoughts, I ask for a round of grog."

"I'm burning up and I'm thirsty," murmured Meurice.

"Here's a bottle for the crying baby," said Mobile as he passed a cup to Meurice, who, being eaten alive by fever, drank it in one go.

"My good sirs," said le Faucheux, "in one month, our association will be at an end. We'll cash out, and speaking for myself, I'll pretend I never knew you. I'm going to Paris, the center of the business world, where an intelligent man is sure to succeed. The best claims, gentlemen, are still found between the place de la Madeleine and the port of Saint-Denis. You can speculate without danger, in good faith and bad. Sometimes a scam changes your monaco into five good sous.

"With money, you can climb the social ladder. I'll soon be surrounded by good wishes and respect. I'll see the world, and the world will see me. Great nobles will shake my hand and grovel before me—or more likely, my wallet. Duchesses and marquises will make my house their home.

"Everything bends under the weight of gold. The stiffest spines become flexible. When Scribe wrote, 'Gold is a chimera,' he was old and gray and didn't have so much as a radish in his pocket.

"One day, when the public's trust, its great shame, is at its height, when my account is full of deposits from all these small-time, naive speculators, I will make my great escape and head for lands where there is no justice. I am the victim of speculative fever. Eventually I'll file for bankruptcy, hand over twenty-five percent, wind up my business, and retire as a nobody, a victim of the impulse I'd wanted to devote to industry, with a few million leftover from my creditors who'd wanted to hang me out to dry!"

"Hurrah!" cried Mobile and Cartahu. "A round of cognac!" And the bottle was passed around.

"I'm thirsty, I'm in pain," murmured Meurice in the delirium of his fever.

Paul was still as a stone statue, his teeth clenched and his eyes hateful.

Cartahu, made dumb by the mines, signaled that he wanted to speak. He stuffed half his hand into his mouth only to pull out an enormous chaw of tobacco, sending streams of black spit into the fire. Using the voice of an English actor, he explained himself thus: "None of these tinkerers are worth a moldy old biscuit. Here's my plan.

"I'll arm myself with a pretty little warship, then I'll press-gang two dozen rogues, real devil-may-care types. I'll risk it. I'll get myself to Guam and look around outside Port Philippe. The first big dipper that goes by, I'm going to lighten my load by a hundred or a hundred and fifty thousand ounces that are onboard, and then I'll sail toward the enchanted rivers." He turned to Mobile and said, "Tell me, Parisian, do you want to be on my ship?"

"Works for me," Mobile answered, "but on the condition that once that's done, we'll go to Turkey. We'll set up pashas, buy zouris, slaves, obelisks, and ride on waves of luxury. I want to smoke a pipe fifteen feet long and only feed on harem sweets, like the Count of Monte Cristo."

"So be it," said Cartahu. "Pass me the brandy."

"As for me," murmured Meurice, "I'm going nowhere. I'm going to die here."

The drunkenness had won out. The songs, the yelling, the gestures, the howls of Cartahu, Mobile, and le Faucheux went on until they were exhausted and dropped to the ground.

The echo of the miner's laughter was still repeating when all of a sudden a phlegmy, nasal voice was heard. A man of fifty or fifty-five, tall, thin, and bony, came forward and stood near the fire.

"*Per Bacco!* You're having fun here. *Buona sera, signori.* Don't get up."

The only reply he got was a kind of growl.

The newcomer walked around with the gaze of an inquisitor.

"Hm!" he said. "We have a feast; we have gold."

This man's features were all sharp angles, and his

small, deep-set eyes beneath an arch of thick brows shone with a sinister light. He was scary thin, and under his filthy clothes, his limbs hovered like iron wires.

He rubbed his hands together and cracked his knuckles.

All he had for baggage was a wool cape rolled up on his shoulders, and in his hand a green fabric bag that held a violin.

"Hold on, old secco," said Mobile, holding out the bottle. "Take a drink, but don't spill."

The stranger took the half-full bottle and drained it in one go.

"What a greedy bastard!" said Cartahu. "That's my master."

"Tell us then, Italian," said le Faucheux, "what do you have in the old bag?"

"*Caro mio*, a *violino*."

"Well, old man, play us something so we can laugh a little. Oh! Let's have a little ball, let's blow a little of our gold."

These three men tried to find their balance on their shaky legs. Impossible.

The stranger pulled his violin from his bag without a word, a violin as black as ebony, bowed and plucked a million times. The strings were frayed and tied in knots.

"Oh, this hick! Tell us, then, you old piece of parchment," yelled Cartahu, "is it sick, your fiddle?"

"Non, can't you see that it's bored being with him? It's yawning all over the place."

"*Pazienza!*" said the stranger as he passed the rosin over the five strings of his bow. "*Pazienza, figli mei*, the instrument is old, but it is gorgeous, you'll see, *pazienza*!" He began to warm up.

"What a rattle!" said le Faucheux. "Hey, Paganini, your beast has a cold."

Without answering, the stranger started to play a sort of rondo. It was very good.

At first the motif was played in all its simplicity, and then the virtuoso began to embroider more complex variations on his theme.

The eye could barely follow the quick movement of his bow. Under his iron fingers, the instrument laughed, cried, growled, sighed. The sound was as plaintive as the whispering wind through the leaves, then whimpering like a baby, sometimes dry and old like a creaking mast, often rowdy and sharp like a diamond cutting glass.

Cartahu, Mobile, and le Faucheux, animated by brandy and dancing, put themselves into weirder and weirder contortions. The bacchanalia continued, the untiring violin was wonderful, the sound grew faster and faster as the spray of notes showered from his bow.

The never-ending rondo shone clear and precise among all the modulations.

Meurice got up from his swoon and fell heavily back down again with a long sigh, and then said the name Constance.

Paul was stiff as an epileptic. The veins in his neck and forehead stood out; his teeth were clenched and his gaze fixed.

The other diggers let out cries and yelled obscene songs. The violin kept doubling its speed.

All of a sudden, then yelling stopped, their legs buckled, and our three fellows fell motionless to the ground.

The stranger calmly put away his violin inside the green bag, looked around himself, took another sip of brandy, and sat still. He looked at the sleeping men.

We left, thinking there was nothing more to see, but we'd hardly stepped away from the smoke when he added pine branches to restart the fire.

Cartahu, Mobile, and le Faucheux, completely drunk, had fallen with their limbs entangled, as if they were still dancing, each with an arm under the neck of the other.

We heard the musician say, "*Pazienza, figli mia*," and he got up.

The next day, as we were setting out on the road, we learned that the miners had been burned by their heedlessness.

The spilled liquor had caught fire to their sleeping bags.

I don't know why the thought of these miners that I saw wouldn't leave my mind.

The barrel was too far from the fire for it to have reached it without anyone touching it.

I wanted to see for myself. I was convinced a crime had been committed.

The Italian had disappeared, the miners' gold had been stolen, and the iron bands next to the incinerated bodies showed that the barrel had been set in between them.

I saw the face of that man. Who knows? Maybe I'll find him again someday.

55

Diary of a Miner (cont.)

We continued along our route through the woods, but we met trouble with every step.

We took paths that I don't even know how to describe to you.

We saw two or three houses or huts made of bark along the route, but we pressed our horses on in hopes of finding an inn that was at least passable.

At last, with night closing in, we came to a fast-moving river. We thought we'd taken the wrong way, and we were sure we'd have to camp under the stars at the river's edge.

M. Malfil... went into the water up to his knees to check its depth while I tried to make out if the road continued along the other side of the river.

I took hold of my courage in both hands, placed my hope in the breath of my horse, and plunged into the river. It turned out to be three or four feet deep, and we found a road on the other side.

All this only reassured us a bit. It did not provide any evidence that we were on the road to Bathurst.

Finally, at nine o'clock, we saw a light and reached an inn.

There was no vacancy. After negotiating, we were able to stable our horses and get beds for ourselves with a meager supper.

The beds were so filthy I won't speak of them. I laid out my sleeping mat, put my traveling cape under my head, and slept in my clothes.

We'd come forty miles so far. Our horses were exhausted, and moreover, my horse's sores were getting worse and worse.

What wonderful types for Jacques Callot, these guys that come through the woods two or three at a time, or even whole families. They camp for the night in the middle of the forest under a tent or in their sleeping bags. While some of them sleep, the others keep watch around a large fire.

Plus, there were huge swaths of forest burnt and destroyed.

When you want to make a fire, you light a tree, then you go off without worrying about the rest. The tree is full of sap that burns, and it ends up falling. The fire catches, it spreads, and it goes on for miles. In the cleared areas, the only things that remain are the tallest trees, which the fire couldn't consume. They look like burned bodies.

I wished to see the face of an intrepid French general in the middle of the woods. He would stop all the miners who passed.

I think that our whiskers made us look like police

officers, because we were watched with worried, pointed looks.

I'm embarrassed to say I counted on being attacked. I always had my little pistols close to hand.

After having spent the worst night possible, we left at ten in the morning.

The stage service from Sydney to Bathurst had come by at nine o'clock.

The road was so muddy that with a carriage and four horses, you could barely make two miles an hour. Carts sank up to their chassis. Along the side of the road in the woods, we kept seeing the carcasses of cows or horses that had been left to die or had been killed along the way.

My poor horse is terribly afraid. For two days I'd done half the journey on foot to settle him. Poor beast! He's my only friend, and I go without eating for his sake.

The rain and bad weather continue.

It's impossible to set out for Bathurst.

We were stopped by a raging river called the Macquarie, which had become impassable, even to swim across. We were told we wouldn't be able to cross for at least a week.

What a horrible night I spent! A night full of sad memories and frightening dreams.

Of course the idea of spending a week here is out of the question, and I cannot give in to the cold.

At twelve thirty p.m., I took my leave. I crossed the Macquarie in a small boat. I tied a long rope to my horse and pulled him across from the other side. It was a difficult swim; the current was strong. After a lot of effort, he made it across.

We again met the guide who had lost everything—horses, carts, and men—and who had been pulled from a creek with unimaginable effort. They call streams that swell during every storm "creeks." Once we'd crossed the Macquarie, we got back on the road to Sofala through the woods.

Sofala is the central outpost for the Turon River. It's a mass of tarp-and-plank cabins. At this point, there could only have been 1,500 or 2,000 miners and merchants in the whole place. It was basically a military encampment.

The Turon is a fast-moving river that twists and turns. Every bend is occupied by diggers who have staked their claims. These claims are more or less next to each other, but there's probably a thousand or more. Each claim is visible from the tent city at Sofala. People had excavated from the high water mark down to the edge of the river.

The general opinion is that the bed of the Turon is very rich. There are people who have been waiting six months for it to dry out a little or be a little easier to work. Therefore, it's hard to find a place to stake a claim, or you have to buy an established claim, and they are very expensive.

It's curious, in any case, to see all these people washing dirt at the edge of the Turon—dirt that they came great distances to find. Some use wheelbarrows, some use shovels to dig holes almost five feet deep.

It's exhausting work. My heart fails me when I see now, up close, what this life and work requires.

However, it's been decided for me. All morning, I walked up and down the Turon to watch, to study, and to try to find an available claim.

I couldn't stay long without doing anything; my money had been spent, and it cost me twelve francs a day to feed and stable my horse.

I'll be happy as long as they don't steal it from me.

I'm looking forward to being in my tent and working.

You cannot imagine the cabins where we slept on planks with a disgusting wool blanket and no sheets.

Ah! Céleste! Céleste! Where have you driven me off to?

All right, all right. Don't let it get you down.

I tell myself, by way of consolation, that all the luxury that surrounds you is paid for by the fangs of misery where I find myself.

This population of miners is entirely made of oddballs.

You see the rejects from cities, low-class people escaping their fates, alongside genteel men who were born into elegance and luxury and who, like me, lost it all. You can recognize the gentleman, even under his red wool shirt and his beat-up straw hat.

Generally, everyone is trying to forget the past by drinking. It's a crude spectacle.

In any case, it's all down to luck in this line of work, and I haven't had any in a long time.

My companion started to complain that it was too hard. I thought he'd leave me soon enough.

I didn't find a thing.

I'd fallen again into depression and discouragement when I met a young man with a kind face. I couldn't place him.

His clothes, like everyone's here, were a red shirt and a straw hat, plus an air of misery and suffering. He spoke very good French and ended up telling me that he had three claims on the bank of the Turon that he owned, and he wanted to sell them.

He wanted twenty-five pounds sterling apiece.

Despite my fatigue and the suffocating heat, I went to see the claims with him.

The property rights for claims are entirely arbitrary. Legally I could set myself up in any empty spot for twenty-four hours and then pay a rent of thirty shillings a month. In this land of the free market, the first comer staked the earth and planted a pole. To stop abuse of the system, these spots had to be taken by force, fists, and firearms.

There are guys who have ten, fifteen, even twenty claims along the Turon, which they have to work. They hold them without paying rent and then sell them on to whoever wants them. It's a good racket.

The three claims offered to me seemed good enough, but I couldn't pay what he asked.

I know now who this young man is.

His name is Mr. Black.

He's a former captain in the queen's army who gambled away his fortune and came to run cons here. He's always drunk, and he loses every bit of gold that he wins or finds.

I decided to do a deal with him for the three claims by paying twenty-five pounds in monthly installments of five pounds.

Afterward, we bought the equipment and tools necessary for our work as miners. It was terrifying how much this cost! With the exception of meat, everything is overpriced. Bread is a shilling per pound; butter and tea are horribly expensive; tobacco eight shillings a pound. In addition, it's fifty percent higher than in Sydney, and in Sydney it's a hundred percent higher than in London. A pair of studded boots costs a pound in Sofala.

As we walked to Sofala to buy our provisions, we met two women, both natives of the Australian interior. They were deformed, with hideous monkey-like faces and legs.

One of them, to whom I spoke, seemed very intelligent. Her only clothing was a wool blanked draped over her.

The way they carry their infants is very curious. The child is rolled up like a snake around their middle, with its head under the mother's arm. Kind of like how monkeys carry their young.

The natives in the known provinces of Australia are generally calm but very lazy, and they do absolutely nothing. They feed themselves on whatever they find, eat like dogs. They eat roots and even the large white worms in the tree bark.

They care nothing about gold.

The famed 106-pound nugget was found near Bathurst by a native, who went to show it to his boss. He received a flock of sheep for it. The boss made more than 100,000 francs, while the native ate and sold sheep for a long while. Today, he's no richer than before. He goes from digger to digger on foot to beg for a bit of tobacco or meat.

They are intelligent, and they can be hired to cross the five or six hundred miles through the forest. You can be certain they'll always arrive.

I hope that tomorrow we can sleep in a tent in the forest.

It's not at all nice, our tent. It's made of calico cotton, and it's in a sad state, thanks to the ever atrocious weather.

Our sleeping quarters consist of a webbed bed with no mattress, plus a blanket.

I can't shut an eye all night. I can only shiver.

By day, I cut down trees because in the woods; everyone cuts down trees. It's the first time in my life that I've cut down trees, and it wipes me out.

Captain Black stole from us in the most shameful way.

He sold us what we could have gotten for free.

My horse, which I'd tied up near my tent, chewed through his rope at nine o'clock at night and ran off into the forest. At least it kept anyone from stealing him. A miner who wants to move twenty or thirty miles farther on takes the first horse he comes across. Then when he gets where he's going, he leaves him in the forest.

You have to be desperate to take up the life I'm leading.

Ah! Céleste! Where have you sent me? And yet I only have one thought, and it's of you.

I only endure this life with the hope of seeing you again and overcoming what happened to me through work. I hope to make you smile again at a passing fancy for the joy of a single minute.

Make the best of this time, which passes so quickly.

If you sacrificed my whole life for some fleeting joy, I will use this life to buy the happiness and well-being that I want to give you in the far future.

Bonsoir.

I kiss your picture.

I'm about to finish my first day of work, and I can't do it anymore.

I'm going to bed to try to sleep. It's difficult with the cold that comes during the night.

Since we're also out in the wilderness, I only have bread and tea to eat.

Today I rinsed about twenty pounds of dirt, and I didn't even net twenty sous' worth of gold.

Gold isn't where we're looking; it's in the bed of the Turon. But it's impossible to work there for another few months due to the water level.

I'm going to dig a hole in the mountains and keep going until I hit rock, as long as my strength holds out, but I'm already hurting.

I repeat: You have to pay very dearly for a very uncertain outcome in taking up this line of work, which you could not even imagine until you've seen it.

Only the miners who've been doing this since they were children can keep it up.

I found my horse again this morning, two miles into the forest. I decided to let him roam free, by the grace of God. When I have time, I'll see where he's ended up and bring him back to the tent.

We're being eaten alive by mosquitoes. It's a real plague in this country. You have to have netting or glasses to work. Without either of those, they attach to your eyelids and over time can even take your sight.

I don't know how long I can keep working. My arms are useless. We don't have any gold at all to speak of today.

All day I carried dirt to the river to rinse it. There was almost no gold.

M. Malfil… didn't do anything at all, leaving all the work to me. I hope that he gets fed up with this life, because if I eventually have the patience to find anything, I'll be the dupe in this partnership.

We're down to our last twenty shillings, and still no letter from France.

In this, as in all things, you have to have a little money while you wait to hit a vein.

M. Malfil… wants to leave. I don't think I can hold on for very long. You have to dig trenches twenty or thirty feet long, at least. I can't do it all alone.

Oh! Céleste! Céleste!

I'm so wiped out I can't even close my eyes.

At least the nights are cold.

I gave a ditch in a creek a try; I hit rock without finding anything.

For two days I haven't had any shoes. I've had to work barefoot.

Céleste! Always Céleste! This name and her memory never leave me. Has she spared a single thought for me since I left?

What am I waiting for from her?

Has she made a single move in my direction in five years?

I'm only her fool and her victim. Now more than ever I'm still her victim.

I forgive you anyway.

No one's working today, so I'm going to spend my day writing and washing both of my shirts.

The exhaustion is starting to make me sick. I feel like my strength is going to fail me.

The solitude and isolation are terrifying.

I am very far away and alone.

Discouragement comes every day, and yet I don't have a word or even a notion of hate toward you, Céleste, you who brings me gladness of heart where I am now.

Not one letter from France! Everyone abandoned me.

We are without funds, and I can't work because the water is too high.

M. Malfil… wants to leave in a hurry. I sold my horse in Sofala for ten pounds sterling and gave M. Malfil… seven, so he leaves tomorrow at nine o'clock in the morning, with the mail.

As soon as he leaves, I sell my saddle and bridle for

four pounds fifteen shillings, and I return to my tent all alone this time, without even a Frenchman to talk to.

I set out all my tools and things and go to rinse some soil in the middle of the river that I took from that same riverbed.

This turns up some gold nuggets, but not much.

I go to bed exhausted, hoping to sleep, but a storm comes in with a flood of rain that penetrates the tent from all sides.

This rotten night is the first that I've had to spend entirely alone.

After an interminable night, cold and damp to the bone, I get up in the worst possible mood. The morning is still awful, and it's impossible to work.

At noon, the weather improves a little. I set up on the claim and write a long letter to Céleste, along with resuming this journal. I'll send the little gold I've collected along with a stem of heather I picked for her in the forest during the trip from Sydney to Bathurst.

The memory of her face won't let me be, even while I sleep.

My God, have mercy on me! Either grant me the ability to forget or the courage to kill myself. But non! I'm trying because I hope to see her again.

Ah! Céleste, may God forgive you, I beg of you.
Robert

After reading this litany of his hard times, I shut myself inside my house, not wanting to see anyone.

My depression was so great, my tears so plentiful—no one would understand.

Poor Robert, who had been so used to wealth, for whom everything bent before his will. Impulsive, proud, and reduced to the status almost of a beggar.

I found him dignified in his misery, and I admired him while blushing for myself.

An idea crossed my mind like a lightning bolt across the sky: I could do for him in a small way as he'd wanted to do for me when he was still rich.

This great misfortune made me forget everything that had happened with him.

I moped. I wanted to open my heart to him. I felt myself becoming a good person while thinking of him. I was proud that he loved me.

I forgot all the wrongs and only remembered the good he'd done for me. After having exiled him from my heart, and not having written to console him, I could recover the stature that he'd lost.

56

Premonitions

My poor Robert,
    I received such a sad letter from you that I now feel so desperate, so guilty, that I don't think I'll ever find words to express to you my regrets, my suffering, my repentance.

My tears are abundant, but what can tears do? What can sobbing do for the one who's caused your own sadness?

You say you haven't received letters from me. They've been taken, intercepted for being unworthy of you.

This is the sixth letter I've written you. The idea that you think I've forgotten drives me to despair. A memory would have done you so much good!

Proving this requires more strength than I have, you see, and I'll go crazy if everything falls on my shoulders without letting up.

You constantly accuse me of being ungrateful—me,

who only lives for you and the thought of you! I don't even have a single thought that doesn't bring me back to you. If you think I'm so uncaring, you'll be even worse off.

But non, your heart must have twisted these words through a lively and often unfair imagination.

As long as you loved me and love me still, I want to have hope. I need this to spark my strength to fight the sickness, the disgust, the exhaustion, and the boredom.

When I receive news from you, I always cry. But these tears are sweet, because I'm comforted by the memory of you.

As far away as you are, my soul is with you. My thoughts, my love are wrapped around you.

You say that I made your misfortune. Well then, I did it without making my own fortune.

I've suffered a lot, you know, but I'm not as high up as you, and I'm no longer looking for respite or comfort. I'll live in my tears to punish myself for having misled you. I'll end up as either a nun or a suicide.

Take care, Robert, because if anything happened to you, I would die. My life is over anyway. It will leave me, just like everything else.

I feel like my soul will wander until it finds yours.

Your family disowned you, you say, but I can't believe it. If it's true, then so much the better. I'll defend you against them, and you will be mine.

I told you that I believe in you, and I put my hopes in God. He alone can give you the strength to endure this misery. I'm going to fervently pray that he will keep you.

I'm sending you heather from France.

I love you *with the purest of hearts. Hold onto a tear, a kiss for me.*

Have courage…hope.
Céleste

I left myself to my shame. My conscience had run out of excuses.

Two things came into my heart: the memory of Robert and the memory of my goddaughter. Her sweetness, her games, her babble, made me forget everything else. I surprised myself by playing with her as if we were the same age.

Being a courtesan didn't allow me to remain alone with my sorrows. Inside this life that I hoped to be finished with, tears and good thoughts are not for sale. People only buy kisses and bursts of laughter.

I was given a role to play in *The Daughter of Madame Grégoire*. This kept me busy. Nights were so long for me when I spent them working.

My ignorance weighed on me more than ever, but my efforts were useless. Studying could not fit into my busy life.

Three months went by without a letter from Robert. My worry became feverish.

I imagined a thousand possibilities. Maybe he'd forgotten me!

This thought buried itself into my heart like the point of a knife.

My God, I said to myself, it's not possible! That would be too terrifying. Oh, I'm losing it...A letter might have gotten lost. It's only late.

These thoughts, these memories, as painful as they are, always help me return to real life a bit.

Every day I made new acquaintances.

One evening, in the artists' lounge at Variétés, I saw a short gentleman in such an odd sack jacket that I couldn't help but laugh, which was very uncouth. I was seeing this man for the first time.

He was very short, rather stout, and his legs seemed too skinny to hold up his body. His head was large, his forehead high, his face intelligent, his eyes lively and bright. He was chatting and laughing with everyone around him, and he seemed to know and be known by all.

I had to go onstage, so I left the lounge.

When I came back, he was telling a story.

I stood in the circle around him like the others, and I didn't interrupt. He was a very funny storyteller.

I asked one of my fellow actors the man's name. She looked at me in astonishment and said, "How do you not know him? That's Couture, the painter who made *l'Orgie Romaine*."

"I know the painting, and I've heard the name, but I've never seen him in person."

"That is a man with a lot of talent, but a very unusual personality. Hold on, he's telling another story. Listen."

I moved closer to hear.

"Imagine," he was saying, "a while ago, I was on the front stoop of my atelier, in the middle of smoking a cigarette, wearing a filthy undershirt, when a carriage stopped twenty feet from me. A very pretty woman stepped out with bags and boxes, and she looked my way.

"'Hey, friend!'

"I didn't move, so she called out again and waved for me to come over.

"If she'd been ugly, I wouldn't have bothered, but she was quite handsome. I asked what I could do for her just to be friendly.

"'Hold on,' she said as she gestured toward her packages. 'Take all this up to my place, fifth floor, on the left.'

"I looked at her, a little shocked. But I picked it all up and followed her.

"When we got upstairs, I wasn't done. She had me put the packages in her house, then she rummaged in her purse and gave me ten sous.

"I took it with a straight face, even though I was nearly choking on laughter.

"She'd taken me for a day laborer. It wasn't her fault; I certainly looked the part.

"The next day, I brought her my card and fifty cents and told her that I was only happy to have been of use. If she liked paintings, she could come with me to visit my atelier."

She adored the arts, and the artist had benefited.

Then he appeared at my side. Speaking directly to me for the first time, he said, "If you have errands to run, I'm at your disposal."

I laughed and answered, "For the same price, I presume?"

"Oh, whatever you like. I don't have a set fee, myself. I'm a good boy. I take what I'm given."

"Great! I'll give you a cup of tea, tomorrow at my place, along with some friends."

He promised to come, and he kept his word.

He is endless fun.

They said he was greedy when it came to his painting, but it made sense to me. His work was beautiful enough to justify the price.

He's very funny. When someone ugly comes to have their portrait done, he says, "Come back in a year. I'm too busy."

The face is a book where he unerringly reads peoples' character. He sacrifices faces for ideas. He'll turn down one paid commission to do another as long as the composition of their face works for him.

Mine must have pleased him, because he said he could draw me, like he had Mme. George Sand and Bérenger.

You can bet I said yes.

This drawing is probably the only thing I held onto because it's signed by a great artist. It took almost three hours for him to make it.

A few days later, I won a trial that wasn't in itself all that important, but it influenced the outcomes of the others. So that no one would be unaware of my victory over my enemies, I threw a party. I was not shy about showing off the drawing done by the creator of *Enrolés Volontaires*. My portrait was a huge success, and its creator received hearty compliments.

Among my memories of the people brought together at my place that night, the first in line is of course Alexandre Dumas *fils*. He was not even close to being the Molière of our time, but he was the son of his father, and his name alone turned heads.

He was a chilly man. His mind was skeptical, deep, and sometimes cruel. But if he said something gracious to you or paid you a compliment, you could believe it. He was not banal and did not throw kind words to the winds.

He had attended the first staging of the *Revue of 1852* and had said to many people of me: "She sang, acted, and spoke wonderfully. If she wanted to work at it, she would have a real talent. Maybe I could write a role for her."

At that critical time in my life, this encouragement meant a great deal to me. I knew that he was speaking author to artist. The fact that I was a woman did not enter into it at all.

If M. Dumas had conferred legitimacy on my way of life, he had also on many occasions put a great distance between himself and my actual person. My stage name had displeased him when I was at the Hippodrome.

I flattered myself in having him as an admirer. Besides, I had already told him that I was tired of all these easy conquests and boring people who gathered around me every day.

A man's talent, it seemed to me, is the most enviable of all riches.

I wanted to live among all these superior minds, but I had no right to that kind of favor. It's only by chance that I had the occasion to appreciate Dumas *père*, Méry, Augier, Merger, Théophile Gautier, Camille Doucet, M. de Girardin, and Nestor Roqueplan.

It's the same with great men as with honorable women. They are accessible to the lowest people because they have basic manners, and they're good and patient.

One name should come to mind among all these names. I don't want to name him, but it is written on my heart and will never be erased. A man above others by birth and especially by merit, he was my good angel, my support in many situations, and he didn't hold himself above helping me with good advice. Upstanding heart, loyal, independent, and free of vain prejudice, he discovered me before I had discovered myself.

They say everyone has their lucky star in the sky. Mine is here on earth.

Robert hadn't written me in four months! Some misfortune must have befallen him.

I went back to my busy life and occupied myself with the theater. Ease and luxury surrounded me maybe more than ever, but the memory of Robert never left me.

It was true torture for my heart.

My little Caroline was my only real comfort. She was an angel of sweetness and health. Her own mother wouldn't have loved her more than I do.

I took her out shopping on the rue de la Chaussée-d'Antin. I was drawn to the gorgeous little bonnets that I saw in a window, and I went in to buy one for Caroline. I took her in my arms so she could try one on.

When I saw the shopkeeper's face, I let out an "Ah!" I was so surprised I let go of the child, who would have fallen to the floor if she didn't have her little arms around my neck.

I recognized the pretty person who ran the shop as my little liar from jail, my friend from the prison, Louise. She hadn't changed. Her face was still so pretty, and she had shiny black hair.

I looked at her with blatant happiness.

I waited for her to recognize me, but she barely looked up. My staring at her seemed to bother her. I wanted to kiss her.

I took her hand and squeezed it. She looked at me, stunned.

I was about to say, "Don't you recognize me?" but I stopped myself short. A voice inside me said, Why remind this poor girl that when you met? The circumstances were as sad for her as they were for you—maybe she'd been lucky enough to forget. That would be better!

She didn't recognize me. I'd had smallpox since we'd

last seen each other.

She was still so pretty. She seemed so happy in her merino dress.

While I was thinking all this, Caroline had climbed up on the counter and was walking among the folds of chiffon. She played with Louise and tried with all her might to put on a bonnet. Louise gave her little kisses.

I bought anything she showed me. Lucky for me, she wasn't pushy enough to show me everything in the shop, because I would have bought it without even negotiating.

As soon as we left, I wanted to cry. Poor little Louise! I remembered her offering me half of her bread. For the first time since that awful part of my life, I thought of it with fondness. The memory of her was like a perfume that rescues you from the jaws about to swallow you up.

I went back to my place, promising myself that I'd return to the shop.

A carriage was at my door. Victorine had been waiting for me for an hour.

"Finally!" she said. "I'm glad it's nothing serious. I thought you were never coming. No one sees you anymore. You're haughty with your friends since your success in the revue. Congratulations. Though to be frank, I thought you were bad in it, but I told you that. What is this?" she said, gesturing toward my adopted daughter. "Oh, my dear, I take back my congratulations. How is it that you, a woman of such imagination, is imitating your fellow actresses? You're wrong; as small as we are, we must be ourselves."

"What are you talking about?"

"What! You're with her at the theater and don't know the story of the little one? But they're talking about it here, in Madrid, anywhere women have tongues. Your friend didn't do anything for glory, all for fame: She read in a newspaper that a woman who was about to die left behind a little orphan boy. She didn't go to the magistrate in person to serve as the child's mother; she instead wrote to a newspaper that published her letter. They granted her custody of the little boy, and she showed him off to everyone. His mother had been dead two weeks, but instead of buying him mourning clothes, she said he was Scottish. She taught him how to act out tragic scenes. When he was out with her in society, she would ask him, 'How was your mother killed?' The child would mime stabbing someone and say wildly, 'Like that, in the chest.' But now the farce is played out, the little boy has served his purpose, and no one sees him anymore. He's been sent off who knows where. Poor child! He's better off, wherever he is."

"I don't understand what you're trying to tell me, my dear Victorine. What I do know is that there is a lot of the snake in you. All your words taste like venom. Your advice pushed me in a direction where maybe I wouldn't have been led astray if, instead of knowing you, I knew a woman with a heart less corrupt, a soul less barren. Skepticism and philosophy are not becoming in a woman. For a time, they could wield these weapons well, but a day came when they wounded themselves. If I have one piece of advice to give you, it's to believe in something. The isolation of the soul is the worst kind of isolation. Beings need belief or love. As for me, I'll never forgive myself for the departure of my poor Robert. I need friends who smooth my rough edges, who polish my mind, and you are definitely not that. You are the exact opposite of that."

"So you don't want to see me anymore," she said as

she stood.

"As little as possible. You bring to mind unsavory memories."

"You'll miss me," she said as she left. "You're just like me. I have ten years' head start on you in becoming disillusioned; be patient! It'll come, and you'll remember today."

She left, and I didn't stop her.

I was thoughtful, worried. The silence from Robert seemed eerie.

Being in the presence of this woman revived my memories, and I fell to pieces again. I had such odd obsessions that I thought I was a little mad.

I saw Robert on a ship wrecked in the middle of the sea. His face was turned toward me, full of love and forgiveness.

I was scared. All these hallucinations were manifestations of the worry and restlessness that overtook me for several days.

Someone rang loudly at my door, and I ran to open it, thinking it was him.

One of my friends had come to invite me to dinner with Maria.

"You're very kind to think of me, but I don't know that I can. I'm in a strange state of mind. If I were a proper lady, I would say I had the vapors, because it passes before my eyes like a cloud that I can't see around. Non, I will not go out today. Come dine here tomorrow, if you like. I'll have some guests."

He accepted, and I was left alone.

I went to bed early, but it was impossible to sleep.

I saw the large picture of Robert wobble, fall away from the wall, and come toward me.

I relit my candle. The picture was still in place.

I went back to sleep. I heard his voice and got up, saying to him, "What do you want from me?"

I listened and didn't hear anything.

Apparently, I'd had a nightmare, but I couldn't shake it.

⁂

At six o'clock, my guests arrived. Since I kept looking at the door, everyone asked if I was waiting for someone.

"Non, but I've been out of it since yesterday. I'm distracted to the point of not knowing what I'm doing."

My guests were fun, and I did my best to be friendly. But my laughter was nervous. I only knew that I wished they were a hundred miles away.

A little after nine, my maid came in. She seemed perturbed.

My concierge followed her and seemed even more upset.

"Madame! Ah! If you knew…"

"What is it?" I said to her curtly.

"Ah, madame, it's…monsieur le comte didn't write to you?"

"What?" I said, standing up in spite of myself.

"Eh, well, madame, he is in Paris."

"Robert!" I cried, suddenly leaving my seat. "Who told you this?"

"Madame, he spoke to the concierge, who told him you had company. So he didn't want to come up. He's waiting in the alley on du Havre."

My tongue was paralyzed.

A nervous tremor came over me and my teeth started to chatter.

I looked at everyone without seeing them. My heart beat as if it might explode.

I wanted to run and couldn't take a step. I had to sit down for a few seconds while everyone stared at me like I'd gone mad.

I wanted to hide, get rid of everyone around me.

I wanted this sorry table swallowed whole.

What! There was a party at my house, champagne fizzed in the glasses, the lights were reflected in the silver plates Robert had given me, and he—he was at my door like a bum. I found the situation abhorrent.

"Have him come up," one of my friends said to me.

These words brought me back to my senses.

"Non, non," I cried as I came to. "I beg of you, please go."

My chambermaid ran after me with a cape and hat.

I saw Robert.

It was really him, but he was in such a state, my God! He'd let his beard grow, and his face was thin and tanned. His eyes were dull, and his forehead pale. Suffering was written across his face.

His clothes were rumpled from the long voyage; however, he hadn't lost his stature.

When he noticed me, he reacted like a man who'd been wounded, but he recovered quickly and lifted his head to look me in the face.

I wanted to kiss him, but he stopped me with a look.

I didn't dare move closer or speak.

He finally broke this terrible silence.

"It's only the dead who never return! You're in the middle of a party, right? I've interrupted you."

"It's unbelievable, Robert. I invited my friends over for dinner."

"I have no right to ask you who is at your house. I should have waited until tomorrow to write you. But you know how impulsive my heart is. I just got into town, and I ended up here in spite of myself. It would be wrong to blame all my weaknesses on you; they're all mine. Anyone who doesn't know how to tame his own weaknesses when they torture him should be more pitied than blamed.

"I fear neither danger nor death. I have energy and courage. Nothing frightens me except the idea of not seeing you again. Oh, you probably think less of me, with your iron will. My weakness builds your strength. Céleste, spare me! Would you be willing to come to my hotel? We need to speak of your affairs."

I followed him without daring to say a word, but he saw perfectly well that my soul was at his heels.

When we reached his hotel, he said, "Well, here's what I brought for you." And he uncovered cages full of beautiful birds in every color.

"Voilà," he said. "I took care of them for four months so I could give them to you. I was cold at night so I could protect them from the wind with my blanket."

I began to cry because he hadn't even kissed me.

He took my hand and said kindly as he squeezed it, "If it were something material you could touch, my love would be worth nothing. I am the lover in your mind. I already told you, Céleste, what I love about you, and it's not Mogador. It's another woman who's fighting to break through your shell."

I wanted to fight, to defend myself, but I was shattered.

You have to pity the defeated.

I kissed his hands. They held the traces of long,

nearly healed scars.

He pulled back and held me in his deep gaze. "If you knew how much I love you, Céleste! Since I've been disowned by my family, I no longer struggle with the whims that carried me away."

"And here I was worried about not receiving more letters from you. I thought you'd forgotten me."

"Forgotten you! I could never."

He lifted his sleeve and showed me my name and the date of his departure tattooed in blue ink on his right arm.

"After writing my last letter to you, a kind of journal that you wouldn't have read, I stayed at the mines another three months. I never gave up for a single moment, but in order to have courage, you have to be in good enough health to keep up your strength, and I fell dangerously ill.

"You can't work the mines on your own, so like everyone else, I paired up with someone, in my case a miner named Faubare. He was French, a former sailor who, I think, had deserted his ship. Despite his roughness and brute strength, he could barely match me, because I was working so hard. The poor boy heard the businessman who had sold me my claim call me 'monsieur le comte,' so he said to me, 'Hey there, Lecomte, pass me my pickax and bucket. Go cut wood in the forest, and make some tea.'

"Since my biggest problem was a lack of proper underclothes, I went to wash at the edge of the river. He asked me if I'd worked in a laundry in Paris. The water still hadn't gone down, the pits were still submerged, and you often had to get into the water up to your waist. This water is some kind of muddy acid that burns the skin. Look at my hands. I have patches up to my elbows, and my legs are literally hairless. All this would have meant nothing if I'd found enough to live on, but all our efforts were in vain.

"When Faubare saw me like this, he refused to let me keep working. I'd never been able to appreciate the heart of a workman, and I must say that they are full of nobility and generosity. He worked for me, brought me everything I needed to my tent every day, and gave me an honest account of what he'd earned that day for our partnership. I told him straight that it was as if I didn't exist anymore, that I couldn't do anything, that I considered myself in his debt. But he wouldn't hear any of it. He sang as he cooked and always gave me the best bits.

"I waited with sharp worry for letters and news from France. I never asked, but it seemed impossible that I'd been completely abandoned. I wrote to Sydney hoping that the consulate had something for me, and it sent me a letter from you.

"I would have died there with nothing to my name but the charity of that brave boy if the young man I had met in London, who was a traveling clerk for a large business based in Paris, hadn't come to my aid. Seeing the state I was in, he said, 'You can't stay here. It's impossible that you don't have any assets in Europe. I'm going to get you ready to make the voyage back to France, and you'll return with goods to sell.'"

"But," I said to Robert, "there was a rumor going around here that one of your close relatives had sent you a thousand francs."

"That's false," he said with a bitter smile. "Actually, I did find a letter addressed to me when I got to London, but it only gave me advice.

"At first I refused to leave Australia," he went on,

"but it didn't take much to convince me that this trip was crucial to my interests, and maybe my entire life.

"When I left, I gave Faubare everything I had: my tent, my tools, my pistol, and the deed to the claims I had bought. It added up to a small fortune for him. Nothing could equal his shock when I signed over the lien that gave him the rights in case of reclamation.

"'Comte de …!' he said as he turned toward me. 'I mean, you are…but I thought Lecomte was your name. If I'd only known! I was brought up in one of your grandfather's houses, and I treated you like a dog from our village. I'm an idiot, and you getting sick was my fault. When I saw your hands bleeding from the work, I should have realized that they were not made to hold a pickax.'

"I embraced Faubare as I cried. Then, inspired by his good heart, I returned to Sydney with this other friend who'd come to find me.

"When the ship raised its anchor, I was sorry to be leaving. That night, when I looked up and saw the string of stars, I thought I was seeing heaven weep over my foolishness. I should have stayed, died down there, but I thought of you. You said to track you down, and I hoped to arrive in time to be useful to you. No one has the right to take back the things I gave you when I was wealthy."

I brought Robert up to speed, little by little, on what had happened in his absence.

He became red when he learned what he'd been accused of. It took me a while to calm him down. He refused to come stay with me in the apartment that had belonged to him. I understood why he was upset. He was too poor to pay his landlord. And I had too much heart to parade him through the streets in the carriages he'd given me.

Without giving him any warning, I put the whole place on the market. The proprietor of the building was fine with one person who'd always envied my apartment, so I was able to get out of my arrangement.

I rented a ground-floor apartment on rue Navarin for a thousand francs a year. I had a little garden for my goddaughter, and this quarter was far enough from the fashionable center to protect Robert from certain neighbors who could have given him grief or made him feel bad for the more modest life he was made to live.

I sold most of the cashmere and jewels I still had in order to live near him without being dependent on him while he stayed in France. I paid for all I owed and a few debts that he had gone into for me but that were in his name.

Robert didn't have a clear enough picture of his finances to notice all these little details. Besides, no matter what I did, he didn't want to live with me. He rented a small room in a hotel on rue Laffitte, but he spent every day with me.

The theater overshadowed him. I loved it so much at the time, and I had attained the heights of success and was almost reaching another level, but I gladly left it behind. It would mean sacrificing something for which I had already sacrificed so much. Friends, high-stakes gambling, narcissism—I let it all go. I wanted to give my life to him.

My personality, my character, were finally revealed in my own eyes.

All my life I'd been so embarrassed to receive, I felt proud to give. I used a thousand little tricks to make people accept these sweet, poetic nothings.

I rebought everything that Robert's loan sharks had

put up for sale: tables, décor, guns. Each thing was a memento for him, a relic from his past. He showed me more gratitude for these trifles than if I had given him a million francs. It was entirely out of goodwill that I did this. I forgot that a great sadness still weighed on my mind.

※

The appeal at the imperial court of Bourges was about to hand down a ruling. I still couldn't sell off my house at Poinçonnet, the pretty little cottage that the people in the area had baptized with the pompous name "the chateau"—the name my opponents leaned on to make a big deal out of it.

It was feasible, actually, that I'd have a little house in the country, but a chateau! That was ridiculous. I had to get rid of it.

The businessmen and magistrates of Châteauroux had known what they were dealing with, so they didn't let themselves be influenced by this terminology. But in Bourges, how would things turn out in the end?

Fear made me depressed.

The big day finally arrived. Robert would have to muster all his courage to show up in court.

I created a version of these memoirs to give to the court.

Robert drew up a document that stated his side, detailing the facts, giving the total amounts I'd loaned him, and defending me with his whole heart. But he stayed in Paris.

What I endured during these three days while the arguments continued, God only knows.

On entering the vestibule of the palais Jacques Cœur, where the court met that day, the cold of the vaulted space enveloped me like a shroud. My teeth chattered, and I was as pale from fear as a marble statue. All the voices around me rang in my ears like copper bells. My name being repeated a thousand times by the echo was searing.

Impatience, worry, and a will stronger than my own brought me to the courtroom.

Hidden behind a column, I heard them treating me with such disdain that I lost my head and let myself slide to my knees as I wept. I forgot the courtroom, the judges. I thought I was in a church, and I desperately prayed to God. I asked him to forgive the past and promised to do better in the future if he would absolve me.

God is good; his mercy is infinite.

I felt calm, and my resignation came back to me. I left the courthouse as I had entered, without being seen. I waited for my case to be decided. I had done well to arm myself with patience. The arguments, as I said, lasted three days and had made more noise than a big criminal case. They came to a close, and the ruling was set for two weeks from then.

I went back to Paris.

The emotions, the shock, had been so vivid that they showed on my face for several months.

Robert begged forgiveness for having exposed me to all these trials, which were more than a typical woman could stand.

That day I was glad for all my miseries. I wanted to have suffered even more. It would have been hard to wait if, as I said, God, who had granted me all my confidence, hadn't also given me resignation.

A week after the arguments in Bourges, my jury trial at the commercial court in Paris began.

Robert owed me about forty thousand francs, for which he'd had letters of exchange drawn up. This money was in fact mine, because the house was mortgaged and he owed a lot on Châteauroux. The court on the place de la Bourse declared that these letters of exchange were acts of indulgence and could not be regarded as binding.

I was momentarily annoyed, but I had placed my confidence in these men. I still had hope even when everything seemed lost.

The lead lawyer for Bourges made a short summary for me. He wanted to make me wither away, to strike me down, to stop the contagion of evil my kind inflicted on society. He wanted to make an example of me.

The courtroom was full. It handed down its decision a week later: a win for me.

This was a good day for me and a really terrible one for my enemies.

In fact, I only had one, but he had looked for some of Robert's small debtors and promised to pay any fees, whether he won or lost. More names grouped together would have given more strength to his case, but some withdrew their names during the course of these endless trials. Others swore that they were sorry to have been led down this path through false reports.

When it was over, the person most interested in my losing had already considered himself the owner of my little chateau of cards and promised reform, change, and improvements he'd make when he lived there. He won the commercial trial, it's true, but that was only the beginning.

I went to file an appeal of this judgment. That threatened to drag on even longer. Then things took a turn I hadn't foreseen.

My house was invaded in my absence by five people working in cahoots on this undeniable violation of my rights. They took, as I mentioned before, any of my papers and Robert's that served their purposes.

I filed complaints with the public prosecutor. At first it seemed no one placed any great importance on the facts. But one fine morning, the turn in this affair arrived. It wrapped it all up and seemed to cause great fear in those who had been laughing moments before.

When those who know the law better than me educate justice, she severely punishes the lawman who abuses his powers. The Châteauroux court sentenced the man to a one-month suspension plus the expense of this unlawful search.

In his defense, he said, "I carried out the orders of an attorney in Paris. I did what he had done himself, thinking that he acted out of virtue of authority."

This frightened the men who, when it came to power, only had what they bestowed on themselves. In light of this, they proposed a settlement that was more advantageous to me than anything they'd offered over the past two years. I refused to sacrifice half of what I owned, though I could have consented just to end it.

They came back humiliated and confused, asking me to withdraw my lawsuits. They sent their friends to me to beg me to stop and offered to immediately reimburse me for the sum I was asking. But I wasn't the only victim of these countless brutalities, and Robert urged me to refuse for a long time, which must have seemed even longer to them. If this money had come to him, he would have voluntarily given it up in the name of reparations. But he understood that he couldn't force me to make such a huge sacrifice, so he gave me carte blanche.

Not only was I free of the responsibility they wanted to impose on me, but I still demanded that Robert's jeweler take on the debts of the young man Robert had so impulsively vouched for. Then, asking them how much Robert owed them personally, I paid everything he owed in his name. The total had risen to more than twenty thousand francs. It was better that Robert owed me that money than those assholes who'd treated him so badly.

In fact, Robert had told me about his plans for the future. He wanted to start a business in some kind of trade. His creditors might have prevented him from doing so. So by my paying those men, just like that, he was free and unchained.

Certainly, spending his money is a big problem, but it's excusable when you have the fortitude to rebuild it. I was quite sure that none of the men I had paid would loan him money in exchange for a promise.

Robert did everything he could to procure the sum required to pay me back. No one helped him escape what he thought of as his obligation to me. He didn't have to do any of this. What I had done only made sense. Half of his debts were taken care of by me, at my insistence, it's true. But hadn't I benefited from his gifts? And what do you do with generosity when it's given to you so freely?

Despite the proverb "youth must be served," the man who is ruined so publicly loses status in society's eyes. He inspires no confidence in serious people, and it seems that whatever is happening at present is what has always happened. With this unfair reasoning, heavy chains are put on challenges that are already so difficult to overcome for those who begin at the bottom in their thirties.

Everywhere he went, Robert found himself face to face with suspicion and disbelief. He asked at one place, he was refused. He went looking for goods to trade, he was taken for a mere merchant.

Often he would turn away and would have blown his brains out if I hadn't rendered a little of that confidence I had in him, a little of that loving energy that always buoyed me in the presence of challenges to overcome.

At last, on the strength of research and perseverance, he found a good negotiator who wanted to help him even though he didn't know him. This man listened to Robert, gave him advice, and promised him goods to trade for a reasonable enough sum.

M. Bertrand (that's the name of Robert's new friend) was a goodhearted man. With his experience, he detected a great intelligence and wanted to do well by this man who everyone had written off as incapable.

When Robert was assured of work, which would be his only income for the future, he asked me in all seriousness to come along to Australia.

He had said nothing about this previously. He'd only mentioned it indirectly, and his request was always framed as "If I succeed."

I swear I had never imagined taking a voyage like that without being scared to death, and besides, I had twenty reasons to say no. If he brought me along, I would still reflect badly on him. His relationships with important people would suffer, and this would lower his chances of making his fortune.

His family was offended and persisted in letting him live in exile from them, which made him so depressed.

But his idea was firmly set. He fought my objections with all the heat his soul could muster.

"You're all I have in the world," he said. "If you refuse to come with me, I won't go. All my courage is in you. My homeland is wherever you are. Who cares what my family thinks? Did they think of me when I needed them? They looked away out of fear that I did need them. Now I'm glad to be disowned, because it set me free. I'll never regret it, and I'll never criticize you for it, but I need you in order to live, like a man needs air to breathe."

I realized I must answer him the way I had already answered him, but I also realized it was useless to resist for very long. Beneath it all, my most ardent desire, my dearest wish, was to never leave him again.

I only had one condition: that my adopted daughter come with me. I didn't want to leave her with anyone else.

His answer was two fat kisses on the child's cheeks.

I told Robert everything I had done in his absence.

However, I did not reveal the existence of these memoirs. They were out of my hands. Not knowing if Robert would ever return to France, I had gotten rid of them when they were done. To bolster my case, one of my friends, M. A..., had asked me to prepare them for him. He read them, was shocked, and circulated them without my knowing. When he had them bound in six volumes for me, they had been read by ten people.

I'll quote a few of their opinions, without which these memoirs would have been doubted. They dictated my conduct and could be seen as an excuse under the circumstances.

The first was M. Camille Doucet. His kind and sensitive spirit was taken aback by these harsh revelations, but he didn't condemn them, as he knew I was contrite.

Mme. Émile de Girardin, that great lady placed by God above all other souls, who is compassionate toward those who suffer and indulgent and merciful for all who are broken, could tell with the sensitivity of her feminine heart that death would be preferable to the moral suicide I'd committed. Though it was difficult, she spent the night reading these pages that had fallen from my hand like tears falling from my eyes.

"It doesn't matter who cries," said the author of *Marguerite, or the Two Lovers*. "We must listen to the cries of those who suffer. I found the reading of these memoirs fascinating, and if ever they are published, they would find their audience among those who understand them."

M. Dumas read them too. His fiery imagination and his extreme generosity made them a reality. He measured in one glance the challenges I had overcome to collect these locked-away memories, put them in order, and share things that were so difficult to say.

The author of *Antony*, who I knew a little, told everyone about these memoirs. He even included a few lines in his newspaper (*le Mousquetaire*) that were liable to pique the curiosity and interest of his many friends.

At this time, I had the occasion to reconnect with a woman whose reputation had made the rounds, probably because she had two personalities and one nickname. One day, she was charming as a house cat, flexible and gracious; the next, a roaring Lion, claws bared, eyes shining, teeth white and snarling, all of it. The resemblance was so strong, the name stuck. This new king of the desert reigned over a corner of Paris for a long time without anyone knowing quite how she was reigning.

The Lion was a short blonde. Her features were as unreadable to me as her personality. There were both lightness of heart and depths of hate inside her. She was empowered by her friends, a high-class crowd that remained faithful to her and opposed to all others.

She did me a favor that she barely even knew about. They say she gets around in society; maybe that's why she has enemies. Who knows if among the most stubborn she didn't acknowledge her debts? I saw too little of her to form an opinion of her true nature.

I like to see for myself things that I've heard so much about. What I'm convinced of is that her mind is one of the most subtle and amusing that I've ever met. It's a ball of fire and filled with grapeshot. No one can escape it, and no one can keep their head.

She knew everything, saw everything, heard everything, and turned it all to her own benefit. She was gifted with an astounding memory, and she knew everyone's story like the back of her hand. Hours spent with her passed like minutes.

No one wanted to see her again once she'd mortally wounded them, which happened all the time. But then she'd go back to being a house cat. She could make you forget with a word or a well-turned sign-off in a letter the deep scratch that she'd given you with a laugh.

A man of intellect who's been her friend for twenty-five years said, "She's a witch or a fairy. It has to be something like that."

This same friend, who we had in common, introduced me to a publisher. I signed a contract. I couldn't burn what I had built out of so much pain. I spent whole days and nights editing and re-editing it. I very quickly took to this constant work and state of retreat. Far from frightening me, the solitude and isolation had a charm I'd never known.

When Robert came back to Paris, he was too late to keep me from entering this new phase of public life—which, anyway, I was entering because of him.

I began to prepare for our departure. This was no small task when you're about to undertake such a long voyage. My furnishings, all that I possessed, had been sent to le Havre when Robert received news that he'd been offered a post that he'd applied for and that he'd given up on getting months before. He wanted to turn it down on my account, but I refused to go with him if he didn't accept it.

There was the question of his future. My own future only worried me a little. I always found a way to work for a living somehow, but him…I would rather have died than see him exposed all over again to the miseries he'd already been subjected to.

I felt some terror in going so far from my country, my beauty, my youth. It would soon be no more than a memory. You can only love things like virtue and merit over the years; to love the aging woman, you'd have to esteem her as if she were the mother of your children.

What if Robert was about to go back to what he'd been—violent, impulsive! What if he was about to get his revenge for having loved me! What if this sea, whose murmuring made me afraid, was going to swallow me! What if, in the end, I could never come back to Paris, where I was born and which I loved like I had loved my mother when I was a child!

Maybe I'd die all alone down there, under the burning sun that eats man and plants alive.

Wasn't the scene he'd drawn for me in his letters

frightening?

In this, as in all things, let the will of God be done! My destiny is to be fulfilled.

Maybe great things were waiting for me on the other side of the horizon, which I couldn't cross in my mind. I'll write to you every day.

May this second journal, if it ever reaches you, be more interesting and better written than the last one.

If my memoirs come out after my departure, Robert will know nothing of it, because we'll be at sea for four months.

And then, who will read them? Just some friends. They'll go unnoticed, like everything boring.

As if the critic will pay them any attention!

Well, to each their own.

I'm going to try, during the course of this long trip, to have the patience of the one who will judge us all. God alone sentences us to the sea!

Fin

www.ingramcontent.com/pod-product-compliance
Lightning Source LLC
Chambersburg PA
CBHW021157160426
43194CB00007B/774